CLASSIC
MOTORCYCLES

The SS80 (this particular one is owned by
Martin Wheway) and SS100 are the best
known of all Broughs

CLASSIC
MOTORCYCLES

Peter Henshaw

Photography by
Andrew Morland

Chelsea House Publishers
Philadelphia

CONTENTS

6 ....Ariel
8 ....AJS
10 ....BMW
12 ....Brough Superior
14 ....BSA
18 ....Douglas
19 ....Ducati
22 ....Excelsior U.K.
23 ....Excelsior U.S.A.
24........Harley-Davidson
36 ....Henderson
37 ....Hesketh
38........................Indian
44 ....James
45 ....Jawa
47 ....Laverda
48 ....Matchless

49 ....Morini
50 ....Moto Guzzi
52 ....MV
55 ....New Hudson
56 ....New Imperial
56 ....Norton
61 ....NUT
62 ....Panther
63 ....Royal Enfield
64............................Rudge
65 ....Scott
66 ....Sunbeam
67 ....Triumph
73.....................Velocette
75 ....Vincent
78........................Zenith

CLASSIC MOTORCYCLES

Published in 1998 by
Chelsea House Publishers
1974 Sproul Road, Suite 400, P.O. Box 914
Broomall, PA 19008-0914

Copyright © 1998
Regency House Publishing Limited

Library of Congress Cataloging-in-Publication Data applied for

ISBN 0-7910-5000-9

Printed in China

INTRODUCTION

'Classic' is a much misused word. It has become one of those words which is often used indiscriminately. We can all define its meaning in vague terms – to describe a design which is so satisfying that it never seems to lose its appeal or something which seems to be in a class of its own whether it be furniture, literature...or motorcycles. It is nowadays used as a blanket word to describe almost any bike with more than 20 years under its belt. It wasn't always like this. In the 1960s, a Brough Superior was seen as a classic bike, but a two-stroke BSA from the same era was perceived as rather more mundane. Nowadays, from Bantam to Brough to Flying Flea and Bonneville, they are all 'Classic Bikes'.

If we have to give a reason for this, then it was the resurgence of interest in old bikes (especially post-war ones) in the 1970s and '80s. Coincident with an interest in old cars, this classic movement gained its own momentum. Wrecks were eagerly dragged from hedges, barns and garden sheds. Magazines sprang up, as did specialist dealers and the inevitable autojumbles. And why not? The whole business has saved many humbler machines which would otherwise still be rusting into oblivion. More importantly, it has given thousands of people a great deal of pleasure.

Neither does it really matter what lay behind it all. It may have been the wistful pangs of nostalgia for a past idealized age in an increasingly insecure world, or a reaction against perceived over-complication of modern bikes and modern life. Perhaps it was that that first generation of teenage rebels suddenly realized they were among the fifty-somethings. With kids grown-up and money to spare, why not spend it on recapturing that misspent youth?

With so many people across Europe and the U.S. getting into the classic scene, it is inevitable that there are as many ideas of what constitutes a classic bike as there are enthusiasts for them. For some, it can only be a British twin like the pre-unit Triumph Bonneville. Others will swear by the animal grace of a Ducati twin, or maybe the back-to-basics appeal of a Harley-Davidson. Others will derive great pleasure from the simplicity of an old commuter, a Bantam or Velocette LE. In short, it's tempting to buckle under and declare that the blanket term is right – anything can be classic. It doesn't have to be fast, rare, beautiful or worth a lot. As long as the owner appreciates it, that's enough.

But is it? There is still a distinction to be made between bikes that are genuine milestone designs, and the rest. Either they were first with a particular feature, or were inspired by a designer's vision rather than mere profit motive. In short, they were different. The Vincent is only one of the more obvious examples – faster and more sophisticated that anything else of its time; the Triumph Speed Twin and Harley-Davidson Knucklehead leap-frogged ahead of the competition; Alfred Scott's motorcycle was one man's ideal. The list goes on – the Vespa scooter and Honda step thru are design classics, even if they aren't classic bikes. Not all the bikes in this book can be regarded in this light, but one thing is for sure. For every single one, somebody, somewhere, thinks it is the best motorcycle ever made.

ARIEL

'As old as the industry' was a slogan Ariel might well have poached for its own use; its first De Dion-engined trike appeared in 1898. That it preferred 'The Modern Motorcycle' was a sign of its forward-looking nature. Other manufacturers have been associated with certain types of engine – Velocette, singles, Triumph, vertical twins.

But Ariel is famous for many different layouts; its Red Hunter singles, four cylinder Square Four and two-stroke Leader/Arrow. There were even conventional twins too. The reason for this lateral thinking where model policy (and the standards of the British bike industry) was concerned, was people. Joint M.D. Jack Sangster (son of Ariel founder Charles) had vision and a good dose of business acumen, managing to keep Ariel alive through the Depression years. Val Page was Chief Designer, with his feet firmly on the ground and a talent for production-ready designs. He was complemented by the young Edward Turner, whose flair produced exciting bikes like the Square Four and sports singles, which Page productionized. With publicity man Vic Mole, and Harold Perrey in charge of competition, it was a strong team.

But this was the golden age of Ariel, from around 1925 on, when Mole and Page swept aside the old designs. Before, a range of undistinguished singles and V-twins, using engines by MAG or White and Poppe, were in danger of being subsumed by Jack Sangster's enthusiasm for the new Ariel light car. This changed

Ariel's Huntmaster twin was more suited as a sidecar-puller than sporting solo. Beige seat and deep claret paintwork are typical Ariel touches

with all-new Ariel-engined singles, a 500cc ohv and 550cc side-valve. The sports 500 could top 80mph, and they were kept up to date with saddle tanks in 1927 and two-port engines the following year. This formed the basis of the Red Hunter range, thought by some to be the definitive British single. The name didn't actually appear until 1932, but when it did, it heralded a sporting 500 with four-valve head (though it reverted to two valves the following year). A 350 followed soon after. One reason for the Hunter's success was its sheer versatility. Right through to the early 1960s, it did well in trials, racing, grass-track and

sprints. It stemmed not just from design, but from the care with which it was put together. Every Red Hunter engine had a balanced crank, polished ports and cylinder head; and the whole lot was bench-tested.

For all their achievements, the Hunters were still strictly traditional singles, which could not be said of the Square Four. Another product of the fertile if fallible mind of Edward Turner, its four cylinder overhead camshaft engine was something else again. Turner wanted smoothness, and achieved it by placing the four cylinders as two pairs of twins, one behind the other. The two 180-

MkII Square Four in final four-pipe form. A prototype MkIII with swinging arm frame was built but never reached the market, which makes this the ultimate production Squariel

degree crankshafts were geared together, and since one ran forward and the other backwards, they balanced each other – firing impulses were evenly spaced and the engine was smooth.

Early, excited reports of road tests spoke of vivid acceleration and a smooth strong pull from near walking pace in top gear. For this first 500cc 'Squariel' (as it became known) was really quite sporty. The engine was compact enough to fit Ariel's 500 single cycle parts, so it wasn't a great deal heavier. But for all the early promise, it seemed as if speed merchants wanted to stick to their simple singles. The original 500 of 1930 soon became a 600, and in 1937, Val Page redesigned the whole thing. Pushrods replaced the troublesome ohc, and the 600 was supplemented by a long-stroke torquey 1,000cc version – just the thing for tugging a double adult sidecar full of family. The rear cylinders could still overheat if you worked it too hard, but the Square Four continued its role as smooth and torquey alternative to a big single or twin. Neither was Ariel's biggest bike neglected – an alloy engine in 1949,

coil ignition the year after and the MkII 'four-pipe' (each cylinder had its own) in 1953. By 1959 though, big four-stroke Ariels no longer had a place in parent BSA's corporate vision, and the Squariel was killed off.

Of the twins, Ariel's own KH, a quiet, fine-handling 500, was another Val Page design. Pictured on pages 6 and 7 is the FH 650, the Huntmaster. It actually used a mildly modified BSA A10 engine (built at the Small Heath works) in the Ariel duplex frame. BSA owned Ariel by this

Odd that one of the most revolutionary bikes on the market tried hard to look like a twin, and succeeded

time, and wanted to rationalize things (which it took to a logical conclusion by closing Ariel's Selly Oak factory in 1963). Despite its mixed parentage, the hybrid Huntmaster was quite well liked – 35bhp was enough for over 100mph in solo form, which also meant 70mpg. Like the Square Four, it was dropped in 1959 to make way for the new two-stroke Leader and Arrow. Given more development, these fast revvy learner bikes might have helped stem the Japanese tide. They didn't, but that's another story.

AJS

Albert John Stevens, with the help of his brothers, built a petrol engine in 1897. It may have been this start from first principles that ensured one thing – AJS always built its own engines. Other manufacturers would buy in from outside, but the Stevens brothers did it

the other way round, supplying engines alone before making their first complete bike in 1909.

Commercial success was not assured though. Despite countless road racing wins (350 AJSs were one-two in the 1914 Junior TT, and won both Junior and Senior in 1920), AJS was driven into the arms of another set of brothers. The Colliers built Matchless motorcycles at Plumstead in south-east London, and proceeded (in the post-war years at least) to badge-engineer AJS/Matchless down to a choice between two different tank colours. They built the business up into AMC (Associated Motorcycles) which became a sort of retirement home for bankrupt bike makers.

Part of the reason for AJS's (and indeed AMC's) financial problems was its over-ambitious racing programme. It had become known, and rightly so, for

The 38/2 was the biggest in AJS's range. In 1938 it cost a little over £84 whether you opted for home market foot-change or export (hand-change) models

achieving racing victories with relatively simple singles. Four valve heads were eschewed, and in the 1920s, the 'big port' ohv 350 and 500 did well enough with an impressively large inlet port, with valve to suit. The overhead cam singles, starting with the 1927 350 and ending with that eternal clubman's machine, the post-war 7R, continued the tradition. But despite the success, AJS would insist on tinkering with complicated prototypes

and racers that promised much but came to little. There was a side-valve in-line four of 500cc, or the complex V4 500 racer. No one doubted that this supercharged bike was fast (it secured the first 100mph circuit in the Clady Ulster GP) but it suffered chronic overheating. This wasn't solved by water cooling, which added even more weight and complication. Its spiritual successor was the infamous Porcupine. Apparently inspired by the Gilera four, this double overhead cam twin was designed from the start to be supercharged. So it was rather unfortunate when the FIM banned supercharging. It was still more unfortunate that AJS persisted with the same design for years with only minor changes – without forced induction it lacked both power and reliability.

But these are the well-known AJSs. While the racers were winning or failing according to type, less glamorous road-sters kept on selling. The big V-twin was first seen in 1910, in 800cc form. It had mechanically-operated valves (atmos-pheric valves were fast becoming outmoded), a three-speed gearbox and (less usual) a kickstart. It was, of course, designed to pull sidecars, an example being AJS's own 'Luxury Sports' torpedo-fronted affair of 1914. It later grew to 996cc (still side-valve), but the real distinction was that AJS made its own V-twin.

BMW

It is a singular fact that BMW, of all bike manufacturers, seems to inspire more rider loyalty than any other – save for Harley. Which provides an interesting parallel. Both have their unique positions because both have built up a unique appeal. No one has ever out-BMW'd BMW, and one reason (perhaps the major one) why it has survived when so many have not is that it offers something nobody else does.

From the start, BMW had different priorities to other bike makers. It was not born out of a group of rider-engineers fired by greasy enthusiasm, but by an ex-aero-engine company, casting around for something to keep the factory humming in Weimar Germany.

Perhaps it was this (designer Max Friz reportedly didn't even like motorcycles) that made the first bike, the R32 of 1923, so unique. There were plenty of people making flat twins at the time, but Friz combined it with a car-type unit gearbox, clutch and shaft drive.

Above all, it was a sensible motorcycle. The rear wheel was easy to remove, the shaft drive was clean and easily maintained and the transverse flat-twin layout meant good cylinder cooling and a relatively low centre of gravity. It wasn't light or fast (the side-valve 500cc R32 could manage only 56mph from its $8\frac{1}{2}$bhp) but it was solid, well-made and reliable. So well did this formula work – with quality and performance above all-out speed – that BMW has stuck with it ever since.

Singles came and went with economic cycles; the bikes evolved from

leaf-sprung front forks to telescopics (the first with hydraulic damping), to Earles forks and back to teles again; there were forays into supercharging and overhead cams. There was even, in the early Eighties, the 'flying brick' K-series. The idea was that these water-cooled threes and fours would eventually take over where the twins left off. They didn't, because BMW's basic, sensible layout, its air-cooled flat-twin with shaft-drive, has been too popular with the punters. It may be a cliché, but BMW's flat twin really has stood the test of time.

The R69S seen here is an amalgam

ABOVE
Gleaming white R69S, familiar to police forces all over Europe, and the top of BMW's range at the time

LEFT
BMW R90/S Racer of 1974, built by Reg Pridmore of Malibu, California, and raced at Daytona, Florida. Many wins from this twin cylinder boxer engine with 90+bhp at 9,000rpm

of old and new. It appeared in 1960, five years after the wholesale arrival of Earles forks, and the 590cc flat twin was familiar to a generation of riders. But with 42bhp at 7,000rpm, it was BMW's sporting range topper of the time – 109mph was claimed, for this, the first production bike to have a hydraulic steering damper. The crank had a damper as well, to quell torsional vibration. The winner of many production races (both the Thruxton 500 and Barcelona 24hrs in 1961), the R69S remained BMW's sporting flagship until 1969.

BROUGH SUPERIOR

Rolls-Royce, naturally enough, has always been jealous of its reputation, which is hardly surprising when you think what the name has come to stand for. So its tolerance of Brough Superior's slogan 'The Rolls-Royce of Motorcycles' says much for George Brough's achievement. His aim was to make luxury high-speed motorcycles; faster than anything else, but quiet, well-behaved and above all, well-made.

After a brief partnership with his father William (whose own Brough motorcycles were slower, cheaper and altogether different to those of the son),

This is typical of George Brough's 'Rolls-Royce of Motorcycles', the JAP-powered SS80

George set up shop in Nottingham just after the Great War. The name 'Brough Superior', incidentally, was not actually George's idea, which didn't stop his father's caustic comment that it made his own bikes 'Brough Inferiors'!

George loved V-twins, great big lolloping, cantering things that never seemed to be working too hard. There were also a few fours, like the Austin Seven-engined, twin rear-wheeled sidecar-puller of 1932, or the still-born flat-four shaft-driven Dream of 1938. But it is the twins which epitomize the Brough. There were sporting overhead valve and milder sidevalve engines, spanning 678cc to 1150cc.

But despite the image, and the undoubted quality, Brough Superiors were (and this is sacrilege) 'bitzas'. The

first bike used a JAP engine, Sturmey-Archer gearbox, Brampton Biflex forks and an Enfield cush hub. Of course, it was all standard practice at the time, but not what one expected from the Rolls-Royce of Motorcycles. Still, none of it really mattered, because Broughs were assembled with such care, a classic case of the whole being more than the sum of its parts. That first bike would surge from 8 to 80mph in top gear, the handling was excellent and like all Brough Superiors, it looked superb. Every machine was individually tested, and not passed until it had been ridden hands-off without incident at high speed. But all this quality didn't come cheap; for most motor-cyclists, the Brough Superior remained a dream.

The SS80 Brough pictured left,

The SS80 (this particular one is owned by Martin Wheway) and SS100 are the best known of all the Broughs

T.E. Lawrence owned one SS80 and no less than six SS100s. This is the last, the one on which he was tragically killed on a quiet Dorset road

was typical of the breed. Like the SS100, its name stemmed from the top speed (all Broughs were guaranteed tested to top speed before sale). It first appeared in 1923, with a £150 price tag which put it well into the exotic class. Power came from a side-valve JAP V-twin of 986cc, and it had all the visual clues which marked out nearly all of George Brough's bikes – a nickel-rich finish, and that lovely tapering tank. It soon acquired a four-cam version of the JAP, pressure lubrication and electric lighting. If the SS80 was a tourer, the 100 was Brough's Bonneville. The ohv JAP gave it a genuine 100mph. This was the bike favoured by T.E. Lawrence of Arabia. His description of a ride on *Boanerges* is one of the best pieces of motorcycle literature you'll find anywhere.

BSA

'One in Four is a BSA' said the slogan, and at one time it was right. Then, BSA it was the biggest bike manufacturer in the world. In the 1950s, it churned out around 75,000 machines each year. Countless people learnt to ride on a Bantam; clubmen could scramble or road race their Goldie at the weekend, replace the lights and number plates, and ride it to work on Monday morning; somnolent riders in stormcoat and waders plodded around on sidevalve M20s; or there were the flashier ohv twins, the nippy A7 and torquey, well-regarded A10. And they were sold all over the world, not just to the traditional Commonwealth market, but to the wide open spaces of a receptive America too.

In short, if Brough Superior was the Rolls-Royce of motorcycles, then BSA was the Ford, being a part of nearly everyone's experience; the British bike industry without BSA was unimaginable. But BSA did disappear, and its collapse in the early 1970s really meant the end of a mass British bike industry. Without it, there was very little left.

But despite their ubiquity and sheer size, BSAs today aren't (with a few exceptions) as sought-after as, say, Triumphs or Nortons. Maybe sought-after isn't the right phrase to use. Every bike has its adherents, after all. It really comes down to image. Triumphs were sporty and agile, Norton had a generation of racing success behind it. And BSA? Dad used to ride to work on one. It went

The Rocket Three lasted only three years. This is a rare (and much modified) Mark 2

on and on; never a moment's trouble, not fast mind, but solid.

The slogan 'Built Like a Gun' reflected that, but it was based in truth. The Birmingham Small Arms Company was a consortium of gun makers, founded in the 1860s, with the aim of mass-producing what until then had been made by hand. But as the demand for small arms fluctuated with war and peace, so did the fortunes of BSA. It needed something else to fill in the troughs. Salvation came with the bicycle boom of the late 19th century, and BSA like so many others took the logical step towards motorbikes. The early machines used other engines, but 1910 saw the first genuine BSA, a simple side-valve 499cc single which was not innovative but was a quality product built, well, like a gun.

The same was true of many of the company's pre-Second World War offerings. Take the 'round tank' 250 of the 1920s. This was the Bantam, or even the Honda step thru, of its day. Simple, reliable and easy to ride, it became the ultimate hack for learners and the telegram boys. It cost less than £40 new, just the thing to help BSA survive the Depression. As time went on, it did get a little more sophisticated; three-speeds replaced two, and conventional front and rear brakes superseded the original arrangement of both hand and foot brakes acting on the rear wheel. One of these bikes took little more than half-an-hour to climb Snowdon in 1924.

The Bantam was its spiritual successor of course, another two-stroke single that introduced countless learners to the joys of motorcycling in general and BSA in particular. Far from being an example of English pragmatism, the

BSA's triple, the Rocket Three, was actually very different from the Trident – tilting the barrel forward a few degrees forward meant different crankcase castings

Bantam was actually a German DKW design, given to BSA after the war as part reward for all the military M20s it had made. There were a few minor changes (the gearchange moved to the right to suit U.K. tastes), but in petroil 125cc form the first 1948 Bantam was much as DKW intended it. Unfortunately, BSA seemed reluctant to develop its learner bike. Apart from capacity increases (first to 150cc, then to 175) it soldiered on in much the same form until 1971. By then half a million had been sold, but it was put in the shade by sophisticated Japanese lightweights. The short-sighted top management, which refused to contemplate any major update, only had itself to blame.

BSA is just as well known for its four-stroke singles. The Sloper (from its canted-forward cylinder) appeared in 1927. It was the first of a line of singles which did a lot to spice up the BSA image, leading eventually to the best all-round sportster of them all. Blue Star was the first, with lightly tuned 250, 350 or 500 engines. In turn they became Empire Stars – foot gearchange and dry sump lubrication made them right up to date. But it was in June 1937 that the Star series reached its apogee. A tuned Empire 500 lapped Brooklands at over 107mph, winning rider Wal Handley the customary lapel badge, a gold star.

Thus came the name for BSA's new 500 sportster. The priority in 1945 was for bread-and-butter bikes, the 500cc M20 and 600 M21 (now lugging sidecars rather than soldiers) and the new ohv B31 350. The latter spawned a warmed-up B32, which was aimed at trials (though in those simpler times this consisted of lower gearing, high-level exhaust, more ground clearance and chrome mudguards). But by 1949, with optional alloy engine and plunger rear suspension, it had lead to the first post-war Gold Star. A 500 followed rapidly, and a new legend was born.

Although the Goldie is often thought of as the ultimate café racer, a bewildering choice of cams, compression ratios and gearing made it clear that the fastest BSA single was designed for competition. Every engine was built from selected parts, and dynamometer tested. It was this versatility, and a very keen price, which was responsible for the Gold Star's incredible success in competition of all kinds. It lasted until 1963.

By that time, BSA's pre-unit twins, the A7 and A10, had been and gone. These were BSA's core range in the Fifties and Sixties. Generally better esteemed than the A50/A65 unit construction successors, the big twins started off as docile tourers, a description which includes Bert Hopwood's smooth-running, strong-pulling 650cc Golden Flash of 1950. And though most A7/A10s were sold as workaday bikes, there were also sports versions, notably the ultimate pre-unit BSA twin, the Rocket Gold Star. Produced right at the end of the pre-unit's life, it married the powerful Road Rocket 650 engine to the Gold Star frame. No doubt it was also a clever way to use up obsolete stock, but it was a high note to go out on.

Only five years later, a sports twin to compete with the Japanese just wasn't enough any more. BSA's A65 came in ever more highly strung (and fragile) versions to keep up with Triumph, but it became increasingly obvious that this was not the way to go. Triumph (now

ABOVE
U.S. export BSA Rocket Three, with small tank and 1971 off-white frame (which was supposed to look like an exotic alloy, but didn't)

ABOVE RIGHT
The 986cc V-twin was a side-valve, of course, and for 1932 came with detachable heads and reshaped combustion chambers said to be worth a 25 per cent power increase

RIGHT
'Gold Star' came to assume a huge significance to a whole generation of riders, and this DBD 34 is one of the last of the originals

under the BSA wing) came to the rescue with something intended as a stop-gap, but which turned into a swansong. It was the Trident – three cylinders, 58bhp at 7,250rpm, 120mph-plus, race-bred handling – surely just the thing to put a stop to Honda's ambitions in the big bike market. In truth, although the triple was fast, and handled, it wasn't quite as new as it seemed. The ohv engine borrowed heavily from Triumph twins, being virtually (as has often been pointed out) the 500cc Tiger with an extra cylinder tacked on.

But owning Triumph meant BSA got its own version of the Trident, the Rocket III. Although mechanically identical to the Trident, its engine was canted forward slightly, which meant the Rocket III actually used different crank-case castings (and made a nonsense of the whole aim of rationalization). But like the Trident, it was a curious mix of old and new. It was certainly fast, quicker than any other road bike at the time, and three cylinders had never before been seen in a mass-produced motorcycle. But there was no electric start, the gearbox had only four speeds and there were drum brakes at both ends. The last, and fastest, Rocket of all only lasted until 1972, when the Birmingham Small Arms Company itself collapsed. Ford had closed down.

DOUGLAS

Douglas was unique among British manufacturers, for two reasons. One, most bike makers were found in the London hinterland or the industrial Midlands – Douglas was based in Bristol. Two, it concentrated almost exclusively on flat twins. So taken was the company (in its numerous incarnations, suffering even more collapses and recoveries than just about anyone else) with flat twins that it experimented with almost every variation on the same theme. There were fore-aft twins, transverse ones, side-valve or ohv, shaft drive or chain. And though the post-war 350 is best known, there were also 250s, 500s, 600s and 750s. The Douglas brother's company was

RIGHT
This Model E Douglas of 1911 was a 340cc flat twin with two and three-quarter horsepower. It had two gears and a free-clutch and, unusually, the engine had square bore/stroke dimensions of 60 x 60mm

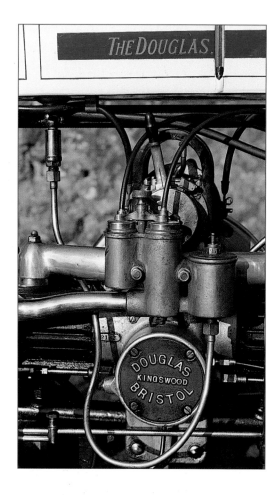

BELOW
Douglas Dragonfly. It was the Bristol firm's last bike, introduced just three years before it gave up on motorcycles

based in foundry work, but did make parts for a Mr. W.J. Barter's Fairy single of 1902-4. This unusual bike (final drive was from the camshaft) was not a success, but Mr. Barter joined Douglas and designed a flat twin, and they were in the bike business. It was the model E, a 350cc bike with atmospheric inlet valve which was made in small numbers from 1907, and bigger ones once a two-speed gearbox was brought in. Although not without its problems (the long inlet pipes iced up and gave poor mixture distribution, the front plug would get wet and stop

The Model E had an atmospheric inlet valve which limited performance to very modest levels. The later two-speed gearbox did help a little though

sparking) there were minor successes in the 1911 TT and Six Days Trial. The 1911 E shown left is typical.

At the other end of the scale was the Dragonfly, introduced in 1954 just three years before bike production ceased. Another 350 flat twin, this one had enough innovations to mark it out from the bread-and-butter bikes. But despite the sporting 80 Plus and 90 Plus (the fastest 350s of their day), it could not survive, and Douglas stopped making motorcycles altogether.

DUCATI

Ducati's 864cc desmodromic V-twin served it well. In 900SS form it had 9.5:1 compression, 40mm Dell 'Ortos, and would rev to 7,900rpm

Ducati may be best known for its sporting V-twins, but these came relatively late in the day. Like Laverda, the Bologna-based firm spent years

making small bikes, until it hit on the winning performance formula for which it became renowned. And again like Laverda, Ducati has survived its troubled existence by fulfilling a demand for something a bit different – a 90-degree V-twin with desmodromic valve gear.

It is important to describe this

desmodromic business, simply because it was so central to Ducati for a decade-and-a-half. Basically a more precise system of closing the valves, it was developed by famed engineer Fabio Taglioni, the inspired designer behind Ducati. In every other engine, the valves are closed by spring pressure. This is all very well at moderate revs, but at very high speeds, the common helical spring cannot keep up with a valve opening/closing many times a second. It 'bounces' helplessly, losing power and limiting engine speed. Taglioni's idea (though he wasn't the first to think of it) was to positively close the valve with a rocker driven off the camshaft.

It was a simple idea which meant more revs and more power. In its first recipient, a 125cc racer in 1956, it allowed up to 14,000rpm, way ahead of the opposition, and enough to secure first, second, fourth and fifth places in the 1958 Monza GP. (A Ducati 125 twin got the missing third place). This sort of success convinced Taglioni that 'desmo' valve operation was worth pioneering. It was to become a Ducati trademark. It partly came about from the light, revvy singles the firm was making in those early years. (It had been set up in 1950, with an unlikely marriage of support from the Vatican and Italian government). They were all bevel-driven overhead cam designs, desmodromic for the racers, conventional valve springs for the closely-related road bikes. They became renowned for speed (the 175 could top 100mph) and lightness.

Not until the 1960s did they grow into the 250, 350 and 450 singles. A simplified (one camshaft replaced three) desmo system brought Taglioni's big idea down

1979 Mike Hailwood Replica Ducati. This is one of the original small batches of bikes with one-piece fairing, Conti silencers and no side panels

among the roadsters. Though fast for such small machines (the original 250 Mach 1 could rival a British 500 on top speed) the later Ducati singles really became legendary for their handling. They were uncompromising sportsters – nimble, accessible performance was their *raison d'être*.

If Ducati had continued to make singles in that vein, it would probably have fizzled out of existence somewhere in the Seventies. Not that it had been blind to other developments. There had been innumerable experiments with the alternatives. There were 500 parallel twins in 1965/66, a 700cc twin (both ohv and ohc, 180 and 360-degree varieties)

and even a monstrous 1260cc V-four. Given its supremacy among singles, the only surprise is why it took so long for Ducati to come up with the obvious development – a V-twin.

The 750GT was announced to an impressed public in September 1970. It took only four months to translate the first prototype engine from paper to metal, an indication of how far Taglioni was drawing on his singles' experience. A 90-degree air-cooled V-twin, with two valves per cylinder, bevel-driven overhead cams, that first 748cc engine set the guidelines for all Ducati Vees for the next 15 years. There were diversions into small two-strokes, and another attempt at

middleweight parallel twins, but they all failed. Ducati learned (and it was an expensive lesson) that a small manufacturer selling at a premium has to offer something different. The vee-twin provided it, so that's what they concentrated on.

There were plenty of other V-twins around, but the Ducati was different from all of them. Moto Guzzi's transverse vees (Le Mans apart) were more touring biased. Harley-Davidson's twin was longitudinal like the Ducati, but otherwise worlds apart in character, engineering and intended use. The Ducati, with its long wheelbase and single-minded sporting nature, was a natural for high speed canters on fast, twisty cross-country roads. That was particularly true of the 750SS and 900SS, which were virtually racers with road equipment. With desmodromic valvegear, and ample torque and power, it was lean and spare in a way that no other Ducati (or arguably, no other motorcycle) was.

But Ducati was not deaf. The old complaints about weak electrics and poor finish were answered with the Darmah 900. Detuned from SS specification, its real signficance lay in the bought-in bits from Bosch, Lucas and Nippondenso, and in the thicker, quality paint finish. In fact, the company, still with Fabio Taglioni as chief designer, proved willing to carry on updating the vees. There were the Pantahs, Ducati's venture (successful this time) back into the middle market, the toothed belt drive replacing bevel gears to produce a cheaper machine. And much later, water-cooling and four-valve heads showed that Ducati would, with luck, keep to its winning formula while remaining in touch with the times.

EXCELSIOR U.K.

Bayliss, Thomas & Co. were first. That is, makers of the first British motorcycle to go on sale. Visitors to the 1896 Crystal Palace Exhibition were offered free test rides on the little machine. It may have had a primitive surface carburettor, belt drive and hot tube ignition, but it was also cheap (about £450) and was even available with smaller 24-inch wheels for 'riders of smaller stature'.

The English Excelsior company never made big bikes, concentrating in the main on small two-stroke singles for the commuter in the street. Take the Auto-byk (the firm was always fond of using 'y's where 'i's should be), more

The 1930s was really Excelsior's golden age, and after the war there were no more overhead cam Manxmen – two-stroke commuters were all it made

Excelsior's Manxman 250, smallest of the Manxman singles. This is the 1936 version

bicycle than motorbike, with a 98cc engine mounted on the bottom bracket. Complete and ready to roll, it cost its owner a paltry 19 guineas.

But the Manxman had no such identity crisis. It was an overhead cam 250, designed specifically to win the Lightweight TT. In its first 1935 form, it had two valves and a rigid frame, but the following year limited numbers of four-valve machines were built, and in 1938 they all got spring frames. There followed 350 and 500 versions, but the little 250 received most attention. None of the Manxmen survived the war however, and Excelsior spent its last two decades exclusively on two-strokes, notably the 250 Talisman twin. It was a pity the 500cc three-cylinder version of the same engine never made it into a motorcycle frame. It stayed in its intended home, the diminutive Berkley sports car.

The American Excelsior's big V-twin was produced in 746cc and 996cc sizes. This is a pre-1924 bike, still with 'Excelsior' on the tank

EXCELSIOR U.S.A

There was not one Excelsior, but four – two unrelated German firms in Munich and Brandenburg (the first built light-weights for a couple of years in Weimar Gemany, the second was a long-lived bicycle maker using proprietory engines); then there was the more well-known Birmingham-based, Excelsior and Excelsior of Chicago.

Like the Brandenburg version, this American firm grew out of a bicycle maker (Schwinn in this case), but its bikes couldn't have been more different. Although the Schwinn Excelsior did make 269cc two-stroke singles and 500 four-strokes, it was better known for typically American big V-twins. By the time it entered the market in 1908, arch-rivals Indian and Harley-Davidson were already well-established, but Excelsior did offer its own ioe V-twins of 750cc and one litre capacity. It also built the Henderson four from 1919, the last of which was a real 1301cc range-topper.

There were problems with exporting the Excelsior though (what with all those namesakes around) and despite being the third biggest bike manufacturer in the United States, Ignaz Schwinn decided to concentrate on bicycles from 1931.

HARLEY-DAVIDSON

Ask most non-motorcyclists to name one bike and they'll come up with either Honda or Harley-Davidson. Honda is understandable. The world is flooded with them, and everyone knows someone with a Step Thru or Superdream. But why is the name Harley so universally pervasive? It's a niche product, and compared to the Hondas of this world production is a trickle.

For some reason, Harley-Davidson has become *the* icon of both motorcycling and America, with all the associated clichés that entails – freedom, power and the open road. It has become the favourite motorcycle for RUBs and BABs (Rich Urban and Born Again Bikers respectively) and in any European city (let alone the American ones) you invariably find a sprinkling of late and shiny V-twins on show. In the United States, rallies like Sturgis, and the factory-sponsored HOG groups are more popular than ever.

It is all a fairly recent phenomenon too. In Europe 20 years ago, Harley-Davidson was seen as the clattering, vibratory remnants of an American bike industry which had simply failed to keep up; you had to be daft or a diehard to ride one. But things are different now, which is why, in a little village in Somerset, England, thousands of miles from Milwaukee, the stationer sells a selection of pens, pencil cases and shoulder bags, all with the Harley-Davidson logo. It's really down to association. Even in its darkest days, Harley was indefinably

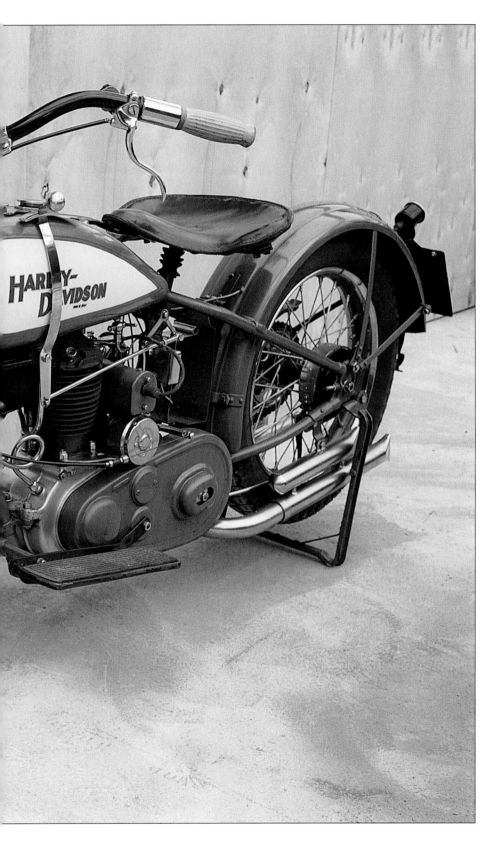

This 500cc 'C' single was one of the rare excursions away from the V-twin layout

American. And in a world where Americana is relentlessly invading the globe, a U.S.-made motorcycle, so apparently arrogant, massive and cool without really trying, cannot fail to be part of it. And the Milwaukee factory, better managed than ever before, has skillfully ridden the back of this Harley-as-style-item wave.

Which is rather ironic, because when William Harley and the three Davidson brothers got things going in the early part of this century, style was the last thing on their minds. America in the 1900s was still a young country; after nearly half a century of development, its industry was fast moving into the mass production age. Incomes were rising and personal transport was in great demand, but Henry Ford hadn't yet brought out his Model T. It was a window of opportunity for American bike manufacturers, of which Harley-Davidson was just one. And it succeeded where countless others failed by putting strength and reliability above all else. It is true that in some ways America was developing faster than Europe, but many of its roads were still little better than cart tracks, and distances were huge.

So when patternmaker Arthur Davidson and draughtsman Bill Harley built their first engine and bolted it on to a heavy duty bicycle frame, they rode it, and kept on riding it until something broke. When that happened they strengthened the relevant part and started again. It was two years before they were willing to take the plunge by going into production, but as news of quiet, solid Harley-Davidson's reputation spread, orders began to flow in. They started out in a 10ft x15ft shed, built by

William C. Davidson, Scottish carpenter and father of the boys. The shed soon had to be doubled in size, and within a year it was outgrown again.

As their company grew, the two friends were joined by the other Davidson brothers. Walter (a machinist) built and test rode the first bikes, before becoming the first President of Harley-Davidson Inc. William, the eldest, had already worked as a foreman, so he was a natural first Works Manager. Production soared once a proper factory was built on Chestnut Street, Milwaukee. It tripled to 154 bikes in 1908, and again to 450 the year after. Then they built over 1,000, then 3,000. During the First World War, around 20,000 bikes were churned out for the army.

Two bikes were behind this remarkable growth. The motorized bicycle had grown into the 5-35. With its 5bhp, 35-cubic inch engine and leather belt final drive, its design was quite unremarkable by the standards of the day. But then, so were just about all subsequent Harley-Davidsons; never innovational, just solid, affordable bikes based on commonplace design. This was certainly true of Harley's first twin, the F model. It is hard to credit now, but Harley-Davidson did not invent the V-twin. When Bill Harley designed one, he was merely following the trend of the times; and this was even more true of the United States than of Europe. Until then, the pioneer American bikes, with their small De Dion-type single cylinders, were very similar to the European ones. But in the States distances were greater, and a bigger V-twin was just the thing.

Like the single, Harley's first twin was convention itself. First with 49ci (811cc) it was soon bumped up to 61ci when the original proved little faster than

'Silent Gray Fellow' was the nickname for Harley's 'F' twin, stemming from the paintwork ('Any colour you like...') and its quietness

The 'F' was Harley's first practical twin – the first one, with its atmospheric inlet valve, proved little faster than the single

This period was quite an innovatory one for the company. Not everyone, particularly the Europeans, used proper chains in 1915

the single. It still wasn't fast (top speed was around 60mph) but was torquey enough to pull a sidecar. In America, these tended to be for commercial use only (ancestors to the three-wheeled Servicars) as the Model T was already making itself felt. It was actually cheaper than a V-twin with chair. Harley and the Davidsons may not have been innovators, but they were quite capable of keeping up with the trends, in pre-First World War years anyway. The year 1911 brought pushrod inlet valves (to replace the antiquated atmospherics), 1912 chain drive and a new clutch; kickstart and enclosed valvegear arrived the year after; and in 1915, a proper three-speed gearbox with optional electric light system the year after that.

But from then on, Harley-Davidson seemed to become rather complacent. There was actually little wrong with the F and J twins, but the new sidevalve Indians were quicker and more up to date. The only substantial changes to Harley's bikes in the Twenties were the bigger 74ci version and the 85mph 'Two Cams'

(each valve had its own cam lobe). Maybe the four partners were spending too long on their latest project. It was the Sport Twin, a longitudinal flat twin aimed at gentlemen commuters. It actually owed something to the Douglas (Harley-Davidson no doubt had export sales in mind). In fact, it is true to say that, apart from the first singles, every bike Harley built that wasn't a V-twin was either heavily influenced by someone else's (Sport Twin, Peashooter single), a straight copy (the Hummer) or even built by another manufacturer (the Aermacchi bikes).

Whatever, the Sport Twin didn't sell well in the United States. It was just too slow and placid for an increasing enthusiast-market. As for the 350 Peashooter single, this did well in competition for a while, but often seized and overheated in private hands.

But it was V-twins that Harley knew best, and it spent most of the 1930s trying hard to best its only remaining rival, Indian. The 45ci sidevalve unveiled in 1928 was a direct response to the lively Indian Scout. Unfortunately, it was too heavy and slow by comparison, though as the W series it did go on to be the U.S. Army's favourite bike, as well as powering the long-running Servicar.

Side-valve versions of the big 61/74ci twins soon followed (another case of following the Indian lead) but it soon became clear that this new V series wasn't all that it promised. The flywheels were so small as to blunt performance over 50mph, and Harley had to redesign the engine's bottom end and recall 1,300 bikes to put things right. Once that was sorted, the biggest ever (80ci, 1,340cc) Harley appeared. That engine size virtually became a Harley-Davidson trademark, as did to a lesser extent, the 61, 74 and later 883cc bikes. Even today, the choice is 883, 74 and 80!

By the mid-1930s, with all four

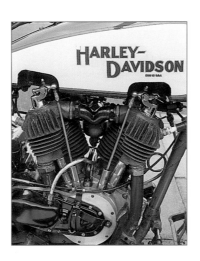

BELOW
Even in 1923, the Milwaukee firm seemed convinced that V-twins should be the basis of its range, and it was right

founders nearing retirement age, the Harley-Davidson seemed in danger of becoming an old man's bike, the tourist's choice. It was reliable, slow and solid where Indians were fast and nimble. So it was all credit to the founders that they recognized the need for a big change, and made it. The result, in 1936, was an overhead valve V which proved to be a milestone in Harley's history – the Knucklehead. Since then, every single Harley twin has been a development (however removed) of this bike. Not only did it have twice the power of the old 61ci side-valver, it looked terrific as well. It revved harder and produced more power

than any previous Harley, had a modern dry sump lubrication system, and Harley-Davidson sold 1,900 of them in the first year. It was a hit.

The Knucklehead was also a symbolic final victory over Indian, which had nothing comparable. From then on, Harley-Davidson was *the* American motorcycle. Still, when war came the Knucklehead was put on ice, and it was the unloved 45 which finally had its day. In full military spec, the WLA was heavier and slower than ever; but it just went on and on, and out in the field that was what counted. Of the 88,000 bikes Harley built in wartime, most were WLAs.

Once the G.I.s came home in 1945, one might have expected Harley-Davidson to be set fair for years of prosperity. It had a huge market share, massive spread of dealers and a pretty good reputation. What could go wrong?

It was first the British who upset things. A trickle, then a flood, of light and nimble twins and singles began to cross the Atlantic. They were not every American rider's glass of Budweiser, but a new generation appreciated their accessible speed, and by 1950 imported bikes had 40 per cent of the market.

Harley did little to the big twins to meet this threat; the new Panhead of 1947 did have hydraulic tappets, but that was about it. Otherwise, it was the same heavy, low-revving, torquey V-twin beloved of thousands. In the years that followed, the engine was hardly changed, while the motorcycling world changed around it. Slowly, the cycle parts were brought up to date: telescopic forks in 1949, foot gearchange in 1952, swinging arm rear suspension (which made it the

RIGHT
The W-series bikes were, at 750cc, the 'baby' Harleys of their day. Slow and unappealing compared to an Indian, their reliability was amply demonstrated in wartime

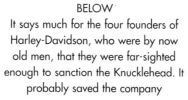

Duo Glide) in 1958. But really, up-dating the big twins wasn't quite so important as finding a credible answer to the middleweight Brits.

It came in 1952. The old sidevalve 45, with its meagre power, hand gearchange and roots in the 1920s was (to put it very mildly indeed) no match for a 650 Triumph. Indian had tried, and failed, to meet the imports head-on with its own vertical twins, so Harley-Davidson tried another tack. It gave the new bike a bang up-to-date chassis (modern suspension at both ends, new styling, foot gearchange). Unfortunately, it was lumbered with a side-valve engine based heavily on the old one. Matters were improved a little by a later capacity increase to 55ci, but it still wasn't enough. The new K series was not a big seller.

The bike it should have been came out five years later. It was the Sportster, another milestone bike just like the Knucklehead had been 20 years earlier. The XL (its official designation) showed a

new direction in two ways. A shorter stroke and overhead valves produced the revviest Harley V-twin yet – it produced 40bhp at 5,500rpm (later 55bhp at 6,800rpm) and was a genuine 100mph machine. Just as important, it looked good; lean and hungry in a way that the big twins never had been. And Harley-Davidson hadn't been completely deaf to dealer pleas for a small bike to sell to learners. The Hummer was a 125 two-stroke based on an old DKW (the same one BSA turned into the Bantam) whose engine also found its way into the Topper scooter. In 1960, it took over the Italian Aermacchi concern, and began to import the 250/350 singles as a direct response to the British and (increasingly) Japanese opposition. Later there were mopeds and 125s from the same source, but in the end they were neither cheap nor sophisticated enough to compete against a Yamaha or Honda.

Meanwhile, things were not going too well for the big twins either. Down to a mere 6 per cent of the market by 1965, the bikes were looking increasingly outdated,

This very early Panhead and matching sidecar was exported to Bolivia, where it was reputedly part of the Presidential guard. It now resides in England

despite the arrival of electric start in the Shovelhead. The factory was under-invested, the dealers dispirited and Harley-Davidson didn't have the money to do much about it. It was time to look for a financial partner, hence the merger (some called it a takeover) by the American Machine and Foundry company (AMF) in 1969. AMF did pump money into Harley-Davidson, but sought to recoup it by virtually doubling the production rate. Quality went downhill fast, and though there were some new variations on the old theme (such as the long, low Super Glide of 1970, and the all-black XLCR, which Harley seemed to think was a café racer) the AMF period bikes got a bad name.

But as the Seventies gave way to the Eighties, the news was better. Quality control was back in hand, a management buy-out regained Harley-Davidson independence, and the company found a rich niche in factory customs. Willie G. Davidson (grandson of the original William) found that his low rider-styled Super Glide had struck a chord, and from then on concentrated on restyles and component swaps. It was a relatively cheap way of producing 'new', different-looking models each year, and it worked. Better still, Harleys were becoming fashionable again, and the truth dawned that all Harley-Davidson had to do was make the bike slightly more sophisticated every year. It need not worry any more about making something really new. People didn't want that – the name and a gently rumbling V-twin was enough. It had to be user-friendly of course; hence the belt drive, five-speed gearbox, rubber mounting, reliable electrics and Evolution engine. But really, the Harley has become a piece of rolling nostalgia, which in this troubled world seems enough to guarantee success.

RIGHT
1962 Duo Glide. Rather than fundamentally change its big twin in the 1950s and '60s, Harley concentrated on slowly updating the chassis. Some diehard tourists resented the Duo Glide's new-fangled rear suspension

BELOW
The 45's writing was already on the wall by this time. Indian may have been on the way out, but there were hordes of faster, lighter and far better handling British bikes being imported

BELOW RIGHT
By 1959, with the Sportster XL in production, the big twins needed to make no attempt to compete with smaller bikes; so they became bigger, heavier and softer still

HENDERSON

For most people the American motorcycle is typified by big V-twins in general and Harley-Davidson (plus perhaps Indian) in particular. But there was an alternative. Companies like Cleveland, Ace, Champion, even Indian, made smooth-running in-line fours which did not sell as well as the V-twins, but served the same purpose. In Europe and Britain, where distances were smaller, the logic behind such torquey, massive-engined motorcycles was not quite so strong – the shaft-driven FN was the only one of note. But out of the American fours, the Henderson was the most well-regarded.

With his brother Tom, William G. Henderson built his first motorcycle in 1912. It was a strange-looking thing, with a very long 65-inch wheelbase and a passenger seat in front of the driver; Bill Henderson believed this was the best recipe for weight distribution. It was only a single speed bike, but set the pattern with quiet and smooth performance from its over inlet/side exhaust valve 1068cc engine.

A pattern for epic rides too. Carl Clancy rode one 18,000 miles around the world, while there were many cross-country records set by Henderson fours. Alan Bedell crossed the States from Los Angeles to New York in 7 days and $16\frac{1}{2}$ hours; Roy Artley broke the 'Three Flag Route' record (Canada to Mexico), covering the 1,700 miles in just over three days.

Meanwhile, Henderson didn't neglect his namesake – a two-speed gearbox came in 1914, a proper wet sump lubrication system three years later. Soon after, he sold the design to Ignaz Schwinn of Schwinn bicycles, who went on producing it until 1931. Arthur Constantine designed an all-new KJ in 1929, with its 1301cc engine, strong five-bearing crankshaft and 100mph potential. No wonder they became favourites with the police.

For American riders who didn't like V-twins, there was always the Henderson Four. This air-cooled example is typical and has not been over-restored

HESKETH

Hesketh, the new British superbike, was announced to a delighted press and public in April 1980. They were delighted because, deep down, almost everyone wanted to see a new British bike. There were one or two sceptics, such as the national daily which described the new V-twin as just another folly of the English aristocracy, but they were in the minority. Two years later, when the whole enterprise collapsed in a highly public and embarrassing manner, there was no shortage of critics.

It was like something out of a novel. The plump Lord Hesketh inherited the family seat at the age of five. At 23, he was running a successful Formula One racing team; now he was going to build a British bike to beat the world. As the plot was revealed, the more promising it seemed. The Hesketh V1000 was to be a one-litre V-twin, full of character, relatively light and simple by Eighties standards, but with all the modern conveniences of a luxury superbike. Engine design was by Weslake, well-known for its race-winning speedway singles, with styling by John Mockett. They were aiming, said Hesketh, at a two-wheeled Aston Martin; fast, superbly-made, and of course all-British. And according to the press (based on brief rides on hand-built prototypes) they'd done it.

So it was a pity when everything went wrong. When the V1000 eventually went into production, the press reports were very different. On bikes intended for sale (as opposed to those carefully assembled prototypes) the gearchange was slow, clonky and obstructive, and there was very bad transmission snatch. Even worse, the engine, that beautiful-looking 90-degree V-twin with its four-valve heads and racing heritage, lacked torque at low revs and rattled like 'two skeletons practising self-abuse in a dustbin' as one of the more memorable road tests put it. After around 170 bikes had been built, the receivers called a halt, though Lord Hesketh did buy back enough tooling to maintain production in a very small way, back at the family seat at Easton Neston.

INDIAN

'The Other V-twin' was the slightly condescending description often applied to Indian. It implied that the Springfield firm was permanently in the shadow of the Milwaukee giant, which was true enough in post-war years. But it is still a rather unfair epithet to what was quite a far-seeing, lateral-thinking, motorcycle maker. Harley-Davidson succeeded through the caution, good sense and innate conservatism of its four founders. By contrast, Indian was first on the market before Harley; it came up with a whole string of industry 'firsts', not just

Indian's four (the first one anyway) was really the Ace, renamed. This 1938 438 uses a 1265cc ioe engine

before Harley-Davidson, but before everyone else as well; while Milwaukee was content to keep the V-twin as virtually its sole product, Indian was willing to divert into fours, vertical twins and singles, whatever it thought the market demanded.

It all started with the classic partnership of entrepreneur/salesman and engineer. George Hendee was a successful bicycle manufacturer, based in Springfield, Massachusetts. An ex-cycle racer, he was frustrated by the unreliability of the early motorized bikes, which served as pacers to the circuit cyclists. When they broke down (and they did) races sometimes had to be abandoned. So when he met Oscar

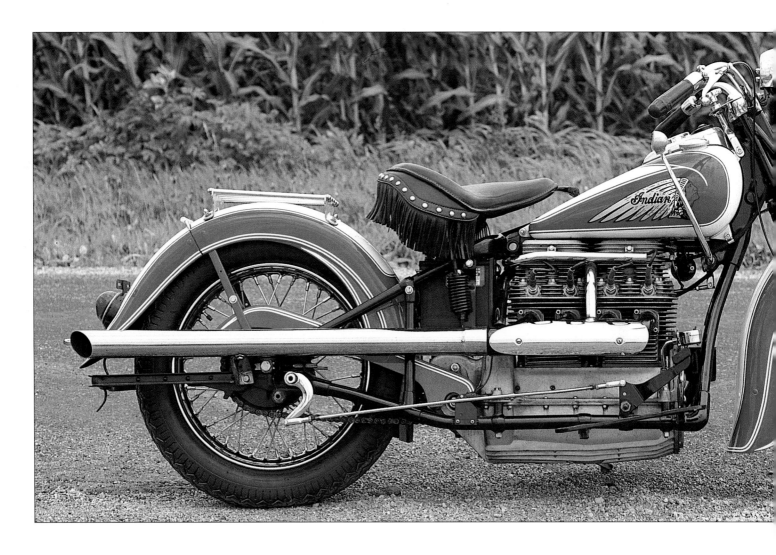

Hedstrom at a race in 1900, riding what appeared to be a motorcycle that actually worked, he was interested. In fairy-tale fashion, the two sat down then and there and roughed out an agreement on the back of an envelope to go into the motorcycle business.

Hedstrom must have worked fast, for the first prototype Indian (Hendee chose the name, and insisted on the red colour scheme) was up and running by early 1901. At first sight, the $1^{3/4}$hp machine looked little different from other motorized bicycles, with its pedals and unsprung front forks. Rather than just being bolted straight in, the Thor engine was an integral part of the frame, taking the place of the seat tube. Drive was not

Indian Chief 80, the company's biggest twin. This 1950 example has foot gearchange, telescopic front forks and a new tank emblem

Indian seemed more willing than Harley to try alternative engines. As well as the fours, there were singles and vertical twins

LEFT
This 1936 Chief still had hand gearchange and a 74ci version of the side-valve engine. The big Indians had always been ahead of the equivalent Harleys, but the Knucklehead was about to change that

RIGHT
The cylinders and heads were cast in pairs, the valvegear was enclosed in alloy, and there was auto valve lubrication

by a flapping leather belt, but by chain. The engine was a single cylinder, with the common overhead inlet, side exhaust valve arrangement – and like most similar singles, the inlet valve was atmospheric, opened by piston suction and closed by a weak spring.

In the manner of the day, this restricted it to around 2,000rpm, and it is doubtful that that first Indian could exceed 25mph, even with the customary downgrade and tail gale. Still, it served its purpose. Hendee and Hedstrom wanted to make a simple, quality bike for the man in the street, and they succeeded. The way to prove it was by competition, which they duly did in the 1902 New York to Boston trial. Hendee, Hedstrom and a rider named George Holden scored a 1-2-3 Indian victory in that 280-mile run. This and other successes had their desired effect, and the orders began to

flow in. Not content with that, Hendee sent one of the bikes across the Atlantic for exhibition at the Stanley Show in London. It was the beginning of a long association with exports to Britain.

Meanwhile, the single was progressing, having been given refinements like a steel cylinder to replace the cast iron and an engine shaft shock absorber to smooth out the transmission. In 1905 came a sprung fork and what must have been the world's first twistgrip throttle. But the big news (for 1907) was a V-twin – Indian wasn't unique in adopting this relatively quick and easy route to more power, though it did pre-date Harley by a couple of years. Being one of the first also meant that the Indian twin developed faster. The $5\frac{1}{2}$ and 7hp versions soon had a mechanical inlet valve and a leaf sprung trailing link front fork. They were chain driven, of course, and had proper

A 120mph speedometer and -20/+20 ammeter comprised the tank top instruments

countershaft gearboxes, which made the Indian Vees very advanced, particularly by European standards. Perhaps it was this advantage, plus George Hendee's continuing determination to break into the British market, that encouraged an assault on the 1909 TT. At this first attempt, on a specially downsized 500cc Indian, Guy Evans finished second to Harry Collier's Matchless, having led for half the race. The following year, 14th place was the best it could do, but in 1911, Indian showed the true extent of its advantage over the single speed, belt drive British bikes and took first, second and third. That success was never repeated, but it put Indian on the map.

But for Hendee the salesman, there were always new avenues to explore. He inspired the Hendee Special of 1914. It was basically the standard 7hp twin, but with electric lighting and starting, the first

ever on a motorcycle. It used a combined generator/starter motor, driven by chain and mounted in front of the engine. Other models benefited from swinging arm rear suspension, which was controlled by leaf springs. Oscar Hedstrom thought the Special was a little too advanced, and left in disgust. He was soon proved right for 1914 battery technology couldn't keep up with the rest of the system, and within a year the Special had gone. Hedstrom did come back to Indian, but not until 1917, after Hendee retired.

While he was away, Charlie Gustafson was brought in as designer, and he came up with the Powerplus 990cc twin. This was a real advance on the old ioe bike as it had side-valves, and stole a march on Harley-Davidson which did not bring in its own side-valve twin for another 13 years.

In fact, the Powerplus's introduction in 1916 was really the high spot of Indian's lead over Harley. It outsold its nearest rival, and was technically well ahead. But things were about to change. During the First World War, Indian turned over production almost exclusively to war work. The result was a great many disgruntled Indian dealers with no bikes to sell. Meanwhile, the canny Arthur Davidson had continued to produce civilian machines as well as army ones, and lost no time recruiting the malcontents into the Harley dealer network. So began the Milwaukee firm's long challenge to Indian for market leadership. Competition between the two was cut-throat in the Twenties and Thirties. One ploy was to gain prestigious police contracts by offering bikes at cost price, and then destroying the rival machines that were traded in!

The Indian V-twins might not be as solid and reliable as the Harleys, but they were a lot livelier. This was particularly true of the famous Scout, the 500cc bike designed by Dubliner Charles Franklin. It was quite a nimble machine, and popular, able to run rings around the equivalent Harley 45. Franklin, who had piloted the second placed Indian in that legendary 1911 TT, later came up with a 1,000cc version known as the Chief, and the 1,234cc Big Chief. These big twins were what one would expect from an American manufacturer. In their classic red finish and all-enveloping mudguards, they were to become the definitive Indians, the 'red steed of steel'.

The Prince side-valve single, just 348cc and with heavy European influence, was different. Another Franklin design, it was an example of Indian's outward-looking attitude to exports and alternative markets at home. The Prince failed to fulfil expectations, but soon afterwards Indian went to the other end of the scale and bought up the four cylinder Ace. Now renamed the Indian four, this 1,265cc machine was a refined and powerful flagship to the range. There was a brief hiccup in 1937 when Indian, for reasons best known to itself, transposed the head layout with overhead exhaust valves and side inlets. The following year though, it reverted to the original ioe set-up, improving it by enclosing the valve gear and using light alloy cylinder heads. It lasted until 1942, the last American four to be made.

The four was hardly the ideal choice for bullet-dodging despatch riders, and most of Indian's wartime production the second time round were Junior Scout 500cc V-twins. The 750cc Scout was not used, but it did leave behind an impressive

competition history. In the late 1930s it became the bike to beat in dirt track racing, largely because of the manufacturer-inspired Class C rules. These allowed 750 side-valves but only 500cc ohv or ohc

1935 four, with hand gearchange. For the discerning, 24 different colour schemes were available

engines, and all were restricted to a 7:1 compression ratio, which further favoured the bigger bikes. Whatever the motives, the new rules laid the field open to Harley and Indian twins. Not that the Sport Scout was slow. In standard form it could top 80mph, and a typical racer with special cams, straight-though pipes and big Linkert carburettor would touch 115mph at Daytona.

But these were the glory days, and things were different after the war. The four was dropped, and Indian brought back the old side-valve twins, but it knew something had to be done to combat the flood of British middleweights. The answer appeared to lie with the little Torque Manufacturing Company of Plainville, Connecticut. It had designed a modular range of bikes along European lines, all with bang up-to-date overhead valves, telescopic front forks and plunger rear suspension. There was a 220cc single, 440cc twin and 880 four. It seemed just what Indian needed, so it bought up the entire project lock, stock and pushrod.

Alas, far from being the quick route to competitive products Indian had hoped for, the new bikes were a disaster. Introduced in 1946, both 220 and 440 (the four was never made) proved very unreliable. Con-rod breakages and magneto failures were just the more common problems. Indian hastily took them off the market, beefed them up, and tried again with the 220 Arrow and 440 Scout in 1948. It wasn't enough, and the little Indians still weren't as tough as even a BSA or Triumph, let alone the big side-valve Chief, which continued to sell in small numbers. In 1952, Indian gave up the small bikes as a bad job, and to all intents and purposes that was its end as a manufacturer. The Chief hung on

for another year, but by now the writing was on the wall.

But it was not the end of the Indian story, which in a way drags on to this day. The strength of the name was such that there were innumerable attempts to resurrect it. First there was the takeover by Brockhouse Engineering, based in Lancashire, England. Brockhouse wanted a firm base for exporting to the United States, and for a few years the Indian name was used to sell the Brave, an underpowered, Brockhouse-built 250cc single. In 1957, Brockhouse itself was bought up by the giant AMC concern (Matchless, AJS and Norton) – Indian became the badge for certain Royal Enfields sold in the States. After a brief period as an import organization for a number of AMC-owned marques (not a success), the Indian name drifted into obscurity.

It surfaced again in the late Sixties, when publisher Floyd Clymer used it to market a Royal Enfield Interceptor-engined bike, and another which used some of the last Velocette Venom power units. A few years later, and we find the Indian ME-125, an American-assembled trail bike with Italian Minarelli engine. Later still (we're in the 1980s now) someone was importing Taiwanese mopeds to the States, with Indian badges on the tank! But even this isn't the end. In 1993 came news that two American businessmen, Wayne Baughman and Phillip Zanghi, were vying for the right to use the Indian name on resurrected, fully-modern V-twins. But with vague plans and little capital, it seems unlikely either of them will succeed, even if the lawyers ever decide who owns the name. Are Hendee and Hedstrom looking down and laughing?

JAMES

One tends to associate James with lightweight bikes, little Villiers-powered commuters of the 1950s. In fact, they were making bikes right from the early days, in 1902, and until 1930 produced a number of four-strokes up to a 500 V-twin. But James started off in a small way as yet another ex-bicycle maker from the Midlands. Its first machine was a pedal cycle with small engine (a Minerva or Derby). Drive was by belt or friction roller.

Although it was never renowned for innovation, the James 'Safety' of 1908 is worth a mention. Instead of the usual tubular frame, this one was open, with running boards instead of footrests. There were internally expanding brakes,

James 350 Super Sports of 1928. This was one of the last 350s. From 1930, the company confined itself to real lightweights only

a leaf-sprung saddle, and the wheels were spindle-mounted, which meant they were quickly detachable in the likely event of a puncture. The Safety influenced other bikes, but was not a commerical success, and James went back to more conventional types. Side-valve 250 and 350 singles appeared just before and after the First World War, and then there was that up-to-the-minute ohv V-twin. It actually looked like a small Brough Superior, and the maker guaranteed 80mph from each one. But it was not the sort of bike to sell in the Depression; from 1930, James made nothing bigger than a 250.

That really set the pattern for the rest of James' existence. There were Villiers-powered autocycles and commuter bikes from 98 to 250cc. Later on, after the takeover by Associated Motor-cycles (AJS-Matchless in other words), AMC's own two-strokes were used as well.

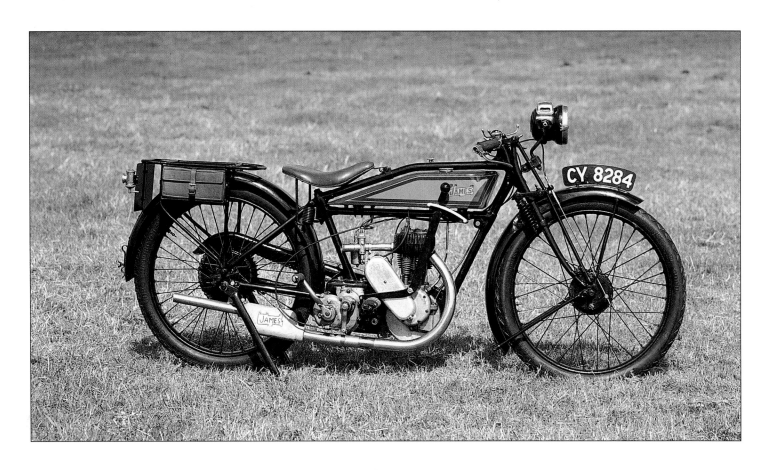

JAWA

Some manufacturers eschewed two-strokes, a few relied on them completely. Jawa seemed to keep an open mind on the subject for almost throughout its history, it has built both. It is tempting to hold up Jawa as an example of strangled free enterprise: pre-war, a promising and free-thinking young company; after the 1945 Communist take-over of Czechoslovakia, condemned to make dull and basic plodders for a grey market. If there is some truth in that picture, it's only a sliver. Jawa had its share of duds before the war, and kept on with overhead cam racers and very successful speedway singles afterwards.

It came to the game relatively late, in 1929, when arms manufacturer

1929 Jawa 500. This 18bhp ohv single was the one Jawa started out with, made under licence from Wanderer. It was soon dropped in favour of an in-house design

One of the last Jawa four stroke roadsters (pictured here in Prague) was this 1955 500cc single. With an overhead camshaft, it produced a respectable 28bhp

Frantisek Janecek decided to enter the motorcycle market. He took what seemed the easiest route, and bought a licence to make the German Wanderer (hence JAnecek & WAnderer). This 500cc four-stroke single looked quite neat and workmanlike from a distance, with its pressed steel frame and shaft drive. It had overhead valves too, which allowed a useful 18bhp. Unfortunately, there were also problems with the valve gear (not to mention the lubrication system and the frame). Despite that, it was light and sturdy enough to do well in trials.

Things improved when English designer George-William Patchett joined Jawa in 1930. He concentrated on racers at first, penning a 500cc unit construction bike with chain drive. Smaller versions with separate gearboxes followed, but Jawa had to wait until 1932 for its first road-going success. This too had a

One of Jawa's own bikes, this 350 sidevalve single gave 14bhp. Like many of the early Jawas it was designed by Englishman George-William Patchett

pressed steel frame, but used a 173cc two-stroke with Villiers-style deflector piston. Cheap and cheerful, this little bike sold well, encouraging Jawa to build Villiers engines under licence. Patchett contributed some four-stroke road bikes as well – 346cc side-valve and ohv singles, and from Czech designer Josef Jozif came a 98cc two-stroke moped, the Robot.

Jawa's happy two-stroke experiences convinced it to develop new ones for a post-war world while still under German occupation – this had to be done in great secrecy of course. The resulting 250cc single, with automatic transmission and telescopic forks, was ready for sale very soon after hostilities ceased. A 350 version soon followed. For the racetrack, there were four-strokes, Skelnar-designed 350 or 500 twins, with or without supercharger. They were succeeded by more dohc twins in the 1950s, which included a 250, and even a road-going 500. But from the mid-Sixties on, it was two-strokes only on the road; basic and good value, but a little bit crude. It remains to be seen, in a post-Cold War world, whether Jawa will be able to regain its former spark.

LAVERDA

If you have the right product, a good reputation can be built up very quickly indeed. So it was with Laverda, which built its first bikes (74cc singles) in 1950, but did not start producing the big, strong roadburners for which it is renowned until the late Sixties. It was really (dare it be said) exactly the sort of motorcycle Triumph and Norton should have been building at the time – a torquey, 650cc vertical twin, but brought right up to date with electric start, chain-driven overhead camshaft and the high speed stamina which riders now expected.

That first 52bhp twin bore an uncanny resemblance to the smaller Honda CB77, but any doubts that it was an inferior copy were soon overcome. Race wins confirmed that the new Laverdas were very well engineered. The bike soon grew into a 750, and sports SF and semi-racing SFC versions followed. The SFC (70bhp at 7,300rpm, 120mph) was more of a racer for the

The V6 was water-cooled, with chain-driven dohc and four valves per cylinder. Fuel was supplied by six Dell 'Orto carburettors – injection would probably have followed had lack of money not scuppered the whole plan

Laverda's V6 was revealed to the press in 1977. Although a racer, it was intended to form the basis of an all-new modular range

road, though the basic 750GTL was becoming renowned as a relaxed tourer.

But it was the three cylinder bikes that really made Laverda's reputation. After a prolonged gestation, this 80bhp machine appeared to an impressed world in 1972. The twin ohc 1000cc triple powered it to 127mph. Not only was it faster than the Japanese superbikes, but it had handling to match. It was known as the 3C, and went on to spawn the U.K.-only Jota (developed by Laverda importer Roger Slater), 1200cc Mirage and the later more civilized 120-degree crank versions. If the SF twin was what the Bonneville should have become, this was the Triumph Trident.

Laverda seemed determined to throw off the early jibes about Honda copies by producing bikes different from those of anyone else. In November 1977 came its most ambitious project yet. The V6 racer was unveiled at the Milan Motorcycle Show, and was intended to bring success in endurance events such as the Bol d'Or. Lack of money put an end to it after just one outing.

MATCHLESS

Matchless was one of the pioneers of the British bike industry. Just three years after the first production powered two-wheeler, Harry and Charlie Collier came up with their own motorized bicycle in 1899. What really distinguished the company from countless others in the inter-war years was that they made a complete range of bikes from a 250 sidevalve to 990 V-twin, and that after initial use of MAG and JAP power units, the engines were all its own.

For the most part, they were a fairly unadventurous bunch – side valve and ohv singles of 246 to 591cc – though there was also the overhead cam racer, the 350 single which was designed to win the Junior TT (Charlie Collier had won the first ever TT on a Matchless in 1907). Despite disappointing power of 13bhp, it remained on the books until 1928. But the real inter-war innovation was the 398cc Silver Arrow. This quiet-running V-twin was yet another attempt to win the man in the

Lightweight, alloy-engined G80s did very well in trials for a time. The name was later revived briefly by Les Harris, who marketed a Rotax-powered 'G80' in the 1980s

The Matchless G80 became one of the archetypes of British singles; not sophisticated but simple and reliable

street over to motor-cycling. With its unitary cylinder barrel and pivoted rear frame, the Arrow was full of novel ideas. Unfortunately, the conservative public didn't agree, and the Silver Arrow faded away after a few years. The same fate befell the Silver Hawk, a 600cc ohc V-four designed on similar principles.

It was a lesson Matchless did not forget, since the company succeeded where others failed. First AJS was taken over, then Norton, James and Francis-Barnett – Associated Motor Cycles was born. Rationalization was the result, chiefly between Matchless and AJS, whose range of conventional, even staid, ohv singles and twins drew ever closer together as the years went by. Still, the parent company showed little sign of ignoring AJS achievements, and the ohc G50 Matchless racer was no more than a stretched version of the original AJS 7R. And the ohv singles did particularly well in trials. In events like the Six Days, the lightweight, alloy-engined AJS and Matchless bikes were for a time almost unbeatable.

MORINI

To nearly all motorcyclists, or those outside Italy anyway, the name Morini means only one thing – small, light, compact V-twins with modest power but superlative handling. But the twins, when they arrrived, were merely the latest chapter in a long-lived firm whose origins stretched back to the 1930s. An odd history too, for in the early 1970s, just when much of the European bike industry was either collapsing, being taken over or undergoing major change, little Morini was thriving. Odder still that the company had no history of making V-twins at all.

Alfonso Morini was a leading light of the original Moto Morini, known as MM, which built successful race bikes between the wars. But Signor Morini obviously thought he could do better, and left in 1937 to set up on his own. With his own foundry to produce aluminium, he was confident he could beat his original partners at their own game. Inevitably, the war intervened (destroying most of Morini's plant in the process) but he still managed to produce his first motorcycle in late 1945, a 125 two-stroke single.

Cheap bikes may have been Morini's bread and butter, but a more reliable pointer to the way the company was heading came in 1949. Still a 125 (it even had the same bore/stroke dimensions), it was a highly-tuned, overhead cam four-stroke. With 12bhp at 9,000rpm, it was quick enough to win the Italian 125 road-race title that year.

Gradual development (higher compression, more power, twin overhead

Morini's simple but effective V-twin was a lesson to everyone. Just as the trend was towards weight and complication, Morini came up with a light, efficient pushrod vee

camshafts) brought the little Morini into contention with the equivalent MVs and NSUs, but it was not until 1952 that it began to win international races. An all-new 175 followed, designed specifically for long distance Italian races, but the ultimate Morini racing single was a 250. Basically a bored out 175, the new bike was developed like the 125. In its final form, it gave 35bhp at 10,400rpm. Still with dohc and two valves (a four valve head was tried, but judged not worth the effort), it could manage 137mph, and provided Morini with the opportunity to beat the early Sixties Hondas before they were fully developed.

Alfonso died in 1969, and with him Morini's racing efforts. Instead, his daughter Gabrielle resolved to revitalize the little firm with a new range of road bikes. These were the jewel-like V-twins which everyone knows about. Just as the Hinckley Triumphs succeeded 20 years later, Morini produced a complete range of new bikes in short order with relatively

little money. The secret in both cases was modular design – from 125 single to 500 twin, they used basically the same crankcase – which kept design, development and production costs to a minimum.

At odds with Morini's racing heritage, the new bikes were simple – overhead valves, and only two of them per cylinder – but the strategy worked. The Heron head engine gave an excellent power/economy balance, and being a small V-twin marked it out from the Japanese. While Morinis were never cheap, neither were they priced sky-high. Road testers loved the handling at a time when Japanese manufacturers still had much to learn about that side of things. In short, the Morinis had character at a time when it looked as though middleweight motorcycles were doomed to an ohc vertical twin blandness. With the following they developed, would it be presumptuous to describe Morini V-twins as the Scotts of the Seventies?

It is hard to believe that the Moto Guzzi V7 Sport engine originated from a mini-jeep for the Italian forces

Despite its origins, the Guzzi V-twin proved to have lots of potential. This is a 844cc version, ridden by Charlie Sanby (jumping Ballaugh Bridge in the 1978 TT)

MOTO GUZZI

Like Morini, Moto Guzzi having had an illustrious racing history, found itself in the doldrums in the late Sixties, and was revitalized by a pushrod V-twin. But there was a basic difference between the two. Morini's racers were always advanced, but still relatively conventional. Guzzis on the other hand, whether road bikes or racing, were always different. It was a sort of lateral thinking: horizontal singles when vertical cylinders were the norm; a 120-degree V-twin against the 90 degrees favoured by everyone else; a V8 racer when no one else used more than four cylinders; and just as the big road bikes were turning to ohc fours, an ex-military pushrod V-twin was used as the basis of a new range.

Aircraft mechanic Carlo Guzzi was the spark, in 1919. During the war, he

LEFT
Thanks to fleet contracts, the traditional Guzzi single hung on into the Seventies. This is one of the last, a 1974 Sahara

RIGHT
Early post-war two-stroke Moto Guzzi. An interesting sprung frame on this one, with twin low-mounted coils and pivoted forks

had teamed up with air force flyers Jean Ravelli (who was killed shortly before the Armistice) and Giorgio Parodi. Parodi's father provided the money, a factory was built by Lake Como, and they were in the motorcycle business. Even the very first bike established a particular Guzzi line that was to last right up to the 1970s. Its 500cc single cylinder was placed horizontally to aid cooling and keep the centre of gravity as low as possible. It had a big external flywheel (the 'bacon slicer') which kept the main bearings close together for a nice, stiff crankshaft. Soon modernized with four valves and ohc, the Guzzi single was winning races in both 500 and 250 forms. In less sporting guise, it appeared as the relaxed and easy-going Falcone, many being supplied to the Italian police. There were of course many diversions – a transverse three cylinder tourer, racing threes and fours (and the unforgettable V8 of course) and some little two-strokes as well – but for some the horizontal single is the classic Moto Guzzi.

Not everyone agrees though. Thanks to the Italian Government, there is another Guzzi archetype. The Falcone was no longer enough for police and army, so Guzzi was forced to come up with an alternative. The answer lay in a pushrod V-twin it had designed for the army years before (it was intended for a sort of mini-Jeep). It did not look very promising, a big, bulky engine (complete with car-style dynamo) in the pedestrian-looking V7. But the next obvious step, the V7 Sport, underlined the fact that this engine was here to stay. Engineer Lino Tonti transformed it. The whole engine was lowered to improve handling, enlarged to 748cc for more power and housed in a long, low frame. Then it was just a case of evolution for the next two decades. There were touring V-twins as well, of course, (notably the automatic Convert) but the V7 Sport became the classic Guzzi twin, leading as it did to the 750 and 850 Le Mans series. In the mid-Nineties, with four-valve Guzzi V-twins on the market, it looks as though converting that old Jeep engine was the best thing they ever did.

MV

MV – expensive, exclusive and very fast. That was the image at any rate of MV roadsters outside Italy – four cylinders, twin overhead cams and shaft drive seemed to confirm it. Of course, there were always those who thought the road-going MVs overpriced behemoths riding on the back of the company's racing success. For racing was really what MV was all about – despite its relatively short career (it entered racing in the late Forties and finally pulled out in the mid-Seventies) ´ MV was phenomenally successful, winning more events and gaining more championships than any other make.

Four Dell 'Orto carburettors on the 750S – only the first 600cc road-going MV used less than one carb per cylinder, but it didn't last long

The original MV four owed much to the equivalent Gilera (it was designed by the same man) but this 750S version was a long way down the road from that

One thing above all else (even above the superb engineering of the MV racers) made this possible. MV Agusta was family owned and run by Count Domenico Agusta. He did not see MV as a profit source, more as an elaborate hobby – he'd always wanted to make the best racing bike in the world, and he had the money to do it. The Count took over his father's aviation business (later famous for its helicopters) in 1927, and built it up into a highly profitable enterprise. That meant, in those pre-sponsorship days, that he could keep racing when other teams pulled out because the profit-led board of directors deemed it too expensive. Undeniably, this was one reason for MV's victory-laden history – no expense spared.

It actually makes an interesting

contrast with Velocette, another family-owned, racing-biased motorcycle maker. The difference was that costs were tightly controlled at the Birmingham firm, and while one half was keen on making racers, the other half yearned to sell a cheap, practical motorcycle which would appeal to all. Agusta sold little bikes too, but for him they were a sideline, (certainly not an essential, money-making proposition) to the main business of winning races.

Nevertheless, it was little two-strokes that set things rolling in 1945. In post-war Italy, the market for the things seemed virtually unlimited, and it was simply the quickest way into two-wheeler production. Count Agusta set the firm up in a little factory in the village of Verghera, and Meccanica Verghera (MV) was born. It wasn't long though, before the Count's wider ambitions became clear; in January 1950, designer Pietro Remor joined the strength. With an ex-Gilera man at the drawing board, what else could MV make but a racing four?

Remor must have been a fast worker for details of the new bike were shown to the press just four months later. It was an unusual-looking machine, with its blade type girder forks and parallel ruler style swinging arm – torsion bars were used at both ends. But it was the engine that attracted most attention. It naturally owed much to the Gilera – 500cc, four cylinders, twin carburettors, 50bhp at 9,500rpm, it gave the 290lb racer a top speed of around 130mph. Outwardly, its only real difference from that other Italian four was the angle of the spark plugs! But despite initial handling difficulties (many changes were made

The America was a little out of the ordinary by MV standards – 790cc dohc four, 75bhp at 8,500rpm, gear primary drive and unit five-speed gearbox. Its price tag matched the specification

over the first couple of years) this first MV four was important, simply because it laid down the basic formula for all the subsequent ones.

Success did not come immediately. The bike wasn't ready for its first scheduled appearance at the 1950 Senior TT, though when it did appear, managed fifth place in the Belgian Grand Prix. Later in the year, something happened which was to move the team up a gear. The highly respected Les Graham, riding for AJS until then, joined them. He was to make a great contribution to the bike's development.

In fact, one of MV's greatest strengths was its ability to attract some of the best riding talent available, men who were often as good at development riding as they were at winning races. Certainly the list of big names sounds like a roll-call of the good and the great of the motorcycle racing world – Lomas, Ubbiali, Amm, Surtees, Hailwood, Agostini. It was sad then, that both Les Graham and Ray Amm lost their lives while racing for MV. The four cylinder bikes weren't the easiest or most forgiving to ride, and sometimes bit back.

But all that talent, coupled with the MV's sheer power, soon brought a whole string of wins. Les Graham was second in the 1951 Senior TT, and won both Italian and Spanish GPs that year. From then on, the tally just went on growing (despite a hiccup in 1954 Gilera won the 500 Championship) as the 500 four was gradually developed. Conventional telescopic forks appeared in 1950; in 1952 there were Earles forks and a conventional swinging arm, and a re-designed engine gave 60bhp at 10,500rpm.

MV's small bikes were doing well too. Just as the 500 was announced, a 125cc dohc single was unveiled. In the hands of riders like Carlo Ubbiali, this became the bike to beat in the lightweight class, and it's worth remembering that not all of MV's 4,000-odd race wins were down to the better-known fours. A 175 roadster was also on offer (a 125 version joined it in 1954) and later developments included a 203cc single and 250 twin, both of them racers. Like the later big roadsters, MV's overhead cam 125s and 175s were worlds away from the equivalent BSA Bantam and Triumph Tiger Cub, in price as well as performance.

Meanwhile, MV was approaching its golden era on the circuits. By the late 1950s, a 350 four had joined the 500, which meant Agusta's firm was contesting all four championship classes. In 1958, many of its main rivals pulled out of racing altogether, citing cost as the reason. Without Gilera, Moto Guzzi, Mondial or Norton to contend with, MV secured the 125, 250, 350 and 500 championships in 1958, 1959 and 1960. It couldn't last. Honda's arrival in the early Sixties put paid to the lighter classes, though MV held onto the 500 title. History repeated itself in 1968, when Honda too decided to pull out – the new MV threes duly dominated both 350/500 classes up to 1972. By this time, the combined might of Yamaha, Suzuki and Kawasaki were too much, and MV's dominance (even among the 500s) was over once and for all.

All this time, small roadsters had been on sale, but it wasn't until 1965 that the first big four was offered to the public. The MV 600 shaft-drive road bike was an ugly-looking thing. With its bulbous tank and massive rectangular headlamp, it was hard to believe it came from the same maker who produced those lithe little singles and twins. The 600cc four cylinder, twin carburettor engine looked the part though, as did the twin front disc brakes (very exotic at the time) – so it was a pity that performance fell well short of expectations. It was far from a road-going racer; detuned to 50bhp and weighing over 500lb, sales were at a mere trickle.

But better was to come. In 1970 came the bike the 600 should have been in the first place. Out went the black and chrome, in came red, white and blue. The whole bike was slimmer and racier. Engine capacity was boosted to 743cc, which gave 69bhp. Strangely, the original's discs gave way to big drums, and the engine's matt grey finish (which became an MV speciality) seemed a little understated compared to the more traditional polished alloy. None of this dissuaded the buyers though, despite a price tag around double that of the average 750. The 750S America followed (788cc and 85bhp) as did a number of other capacity stretches – first to 832cc, then 862 and finally 955. Like everyone else, MV was obliged to keep up in the horsepower race, whether or not it was being run for profit.

The first MV 600 roadster used black and chrome, which did nothing to enhance its already ungainly appearance. The blue tank and red seat of this 750S are more typical MV

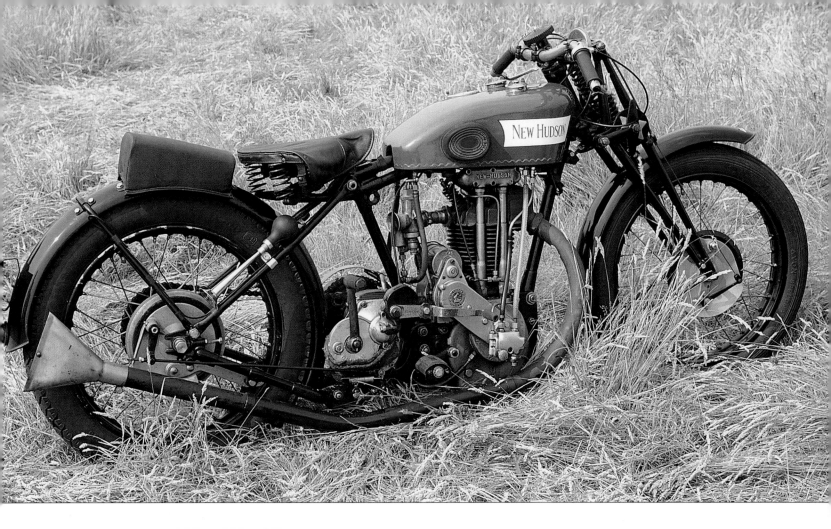

NEW HUDSON

New Hudson made mainly small bikes, so this 500 was the flagship of the range in the 1920s

Like Douglas, New Hudson was eventually bought up by BSA, its name ending up on what was basically a BSA-built moped. In fact, the company only stood on its own up until 1933, though it had had 24 years of independence before that. Established in 1909, it benefited from a close association with two well-known rider-designers, Fred Hutton and Bert Le Vack.

These were the days when a bike's designer would often prove it at weekends by riding in the nearest competition – Harley-Davidson started out in this way. Racing success attracted other riders like Jimmy Guthrie and Tom Bullus to New Hudson, while Le Vack made a speciality of record-breaking at Brooklands.

Unlike many small manufacturers, New Hudson actually built many of its own engines. They were singles, side-valve or ohv four-strokes of 346, 496 or 598cc, though there was also a small two-stroke. This 211cc machine was produced at around the time of the Great War, and featured a two-speed gearbox with the choice of chain or belt drive. It was actually part of a big range at the time, as New Hudson sold big V-twins as well, plus MAG-engined three-wheelers.

Alas, despite the big range, racing success and experiments in the 1920s with full enclosure for engine and gearbox, New Hudson could not withstand the Depression, and production ceased in 1933. Nothing else carried the name until 1945, when BSA resurrected it for a 98cc Villiers-powered commuter. Surprisingly, New Hudson survived in this form up to 1957.

NEW IMPERIAL

Like Matchless, New Imperial made its own engines, though up until 1925 used Precision and JAP units as well. Most of these were singles, such as the 146cc ohv, but there were 250 and 350 overhead valvers as well, with a 500 V-twin to head the early 1920s range. There was also some racing experience with the V, which was supercharged for 1934/5. It was, by all accounts, extremely fast, but even the famous Stanley Woods admitted that it was a bit too much of a handful in road races.

But primarily, New Imperial made small, relatively cheap motorcycles. Although it had survived the Depression, it was by no means in good shape as the 1930s progressed, and was swallowed up in the end by Ariel/Triumph. Jack Sangster's Triumph was then riding on

The Twenties was really New Imperial's last fling at independence. Once taken over by Jack Sangster's Ariel/Triumph combine, it soon disappeared

the crest of a wave after the great reception for its new Speed Twin, but needed a small single to sell below the bigger bikes. It seemed like the ideal solution, as New Imperial's 147cc Unit Minor was a good-looking and well-thought-of little bike.

As Bert Hopwood (then Edward Turner's design assistant at Triumph) later recalled, it would have been easy to simply transfer production to Triumph's own factory in Coventry. Unfortunately, the persuasive Edward Turner had his way, and went about designing an all-new New Imperial. A prototype was on the road after just six months, the idea being that it would share some components with the planned 3TU Triumph. It was all pretty academic, as the war intervened to make production of existing bikes more important. The New Imperial factory was sold to another firm to concentrate on war work, and the name was no more.

NORTON

Norton – arguably the most instantly recognizable and evocative name of all British bikes. But despite being seen (with BSA and Triumph) as one of the big three, it was not a big concern. In the Fifties, production was around one-eighth of BSA's. It was tremendous racing success over a long period which secured the Norton name its place of respect.

Time and again, Norton (or more often, someone outside the company) would come up with something that

1939 ES2, one of Norton's long-running favourites. It was the overhead valve version of the familiar long stroke (79 x 100mm) 500, and continued almost unchanged after the war

enabled a leap ahead of the opposition. In the 1930s, it was of course the overhead camshaft engine, powering the Inter or 'cammy' Norton to domination of the TT. After the war, the McCandless brothers came up with the famous Featherbed frame, whose handling abilities allowed the now ageing ohc engine to keep ahead of track rivals. To a lesser extent, Peter Williams' Commando-engined monocoque bike of 1973 did the same job. Finally, in the 1980s, just as everyone thought it was all over, Norton came back with the rotary engine for more race wins.

But despite the victories, Norton had a major on-going problem for most of its life – it was perennially short of money. In fact, it is true to say that this was not *despite* the competition success at all, but *because* of it. The company was so racing biased that for many years resources were poured into the competition department, to the detriment of bread and butter road bikes that made racing possible in the first place. No one makes a big profit from selling racing bikes.

Perhaps it was a mixed blessing then, that a Norton won the first ever TT in 1907. Ridden by Rem Fowler, the Peugeot-engined bike won the twin cylinder class. Maybe it was this win that encouraged James Lansdowne Norton to build his first in-house engine the

1936 International in the heyday of its TT success. This 490cc Model 30 cleaned up the Senior, and the 348cc version did the same in the Junior

following year. He had started business in 1898, making parts for bicycles, before progressing to the inevitable motorized pushbike in 1902. At first, proprietory engines from Clemet, Moto-Rêve and (as on the TT winner) Peugeot were fitted. The first proper Norton engine was to highlight another aspect of the firm – once it designed something, it tended to stay in production for a long, long time. This was more true of that first 633cc single than any other. Incredibly, it was to survive up to 1954.

This thumping side-valver (known as the Big Four) was soon joined by the smaller 490cc 16H (which came in both side-valve and ohv forms). Like its

sidecar-pulling stable mate, the 16H was a price list fixture for years. There were successes in the TT and the Auto-Cycle Union's reliability trials (one of which involved climbing Mount Snowdon 100 times without a break!) But it was the new overhead camshaft single of 1927 that brought TT domination; between 1931 and 1938 it won almost every single TT race. In Europe too, and even at the American Daytona races (where the rules were biased against smaller-engined, advanced bikes) the cammy Norton made its mark. After the war, the racing department under Joe Craig sought to keep all this going by squeezing out a little more power each year, in the face of modern multi-cylinder opposition.

The downside of all this was a Norton hallmark – neglect of the road bikes. When Bert Hopwood (ex-Ariel and Triumph) joined in 1947, he was astonished at what he found. The factory in Bracebridge Street was a ramshackle place, leaky and vermin-infested, and had grown up higgledy-piggledy as the business expanded. The bikes it made were outdated, oily, noisy singles which sold purely on the glamour of racing success.

His answer was the Dominator, an up-to-date 500 vertical twin to rival Triumph, BSA and everyone else who was jumping on the twin cylinder bandwagon. It cost more than the equivalent Triumph, but was really one of the better Speed Twin-inspired engines, benefiting from Hopwood's experience with Edward Turner's machine. Hence the splayed valve gear and single camshaft at the rear, both designed to help cooling. This engine was to be Norton's backbone for the next 30

The Manx was Norton's ultimate ohc single, maybe **the** ultimate, born in the late Twenties and developed for over 20 years

RIGHT
The Dominator was Norton's admission (rather reluctant) that it could not survive on its age-old singles alone

years, growing ever bigger and more powerful to meet the demands for ever more performance.

First it became the 600cc 99, then there was the 650cc twin carburettor Manxman. Between the two, higher tuned 88SS and 99SS Dominators intervened. The 750cc Atlas of 1962 was at first offered only in softly tuned single carburettor form; but inevitably, the compression went up and it gained another carburettor. In the Commando, the level of tuning continued to increase

noise than the paying public was prepared to pay for. Only with the extensively redesigned 850 twin in 1973 did Norton seem to accept that a pushrod twin just couldn't cut it as a sports engine any more. And the 850, lower revving and less heavily stressed, did indeed prove more reliable than the 750.

But chassis design was more significant than engines in the postwar Norton story. In a classic case of racing improving the breed, the McCandless brothers' Featherbed frame was transferred from racing special to standard wear for nearly all the road-going bikes. That was partly made possible by Rex McCandless's determination to make the frame relatively simple and cheap to build. Just as important, it was stiff and strong enough to produce superlative handling (better than anything from Triumph and BSA); there were no long, unsupported tubes, and new welding techniques meant it was lighter as well. Little wonder that it became the favourite of all builders of specials – the Triton married the Featherbed with Triumph's tuneable twin.

in the face of the now mainly Japanese competition. This peaked with the infamous Combat motor, which had plenty of power straight out of the showroom but rarely stayed in one piece for very long. In other words, an engine designed as a 29bhp 500 was now being asked to cope with 750cc and 50 per cent more power. Just like the outmoded singles it had been designed to replace (though they actually struggled on into the Sixties), the Norton twin was suffering from more vibration, leaks and

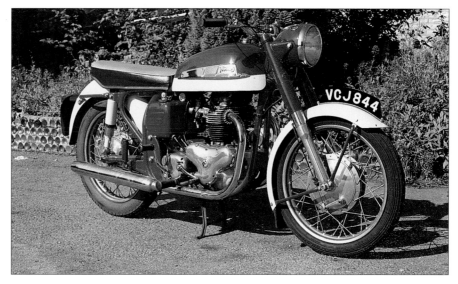

The Featherbed was a great success, but its successor came about for different reasons. The new Commando's Isolastic system was a method of rubber mounting the engine, gearbox and swinging arm to eliminate vibration felt by the rider. It was ingenious in its own way (and won a Castrol design award in 1970) but seemed suspiciously like treating the symptoms rather than effecting a cure. Everyone agreed that the big 750 vibrated too much, and the obvious answer was to design a new up-to-date engine. In reality, it was probably shortage of money that led to a means of diverting vibration rather than eliminating it. And none of this should detract from the Commando itself. It was a match for the BSA/Triumph triples on speed (probably slightly quicker from low revs), handled well (as long as the Isolastics were properly adjusted) and really did mean a vibe-free ride (above very low speeds).

Unfortunately, none of this was enough to ensure its survival in the mid-

Like all ohc Nortons, the Manx was the glamorous flagship racer, intended to reflect glory on the lowlier roadsters. Unfortunately, racing became an end in itself for Bracebridge Street

At the other end of the Norton twin line was this last Commando 850 MkIII. This final engine was more reliable than the highly stressed 750s, though the electric start was revealingly called an 'electrical assister' by the factory

1970s. As even the long-running police contracts dried up, so did sales of the Commando, and Norton went into virtual hibernation for a few years. When the long-awaited rotary-engined bike finally arrived, it was for police use only. As ever, lack of money held back a public launch, and despite a final burst of competition success, under-funded Norton could not survive as a motorcycle maker. Even as this is written, the company keeps up a precarious living, on spares and servicing. Will it make yet another come-back? It has happened before.

NUT

Most of the British bike manufacturers featured here, the reader cannot have failed to notice, hailed from the Midlands, from Coventry or Birmingham. But NUT drew its name from the initials of its home town – Newcastle-Upon-Tyne. Its life was not a long one, arriving (in pioneer terms) relatively late in 1912 and being killed off by the Depression in the early 1930s. But it managed a TT win in that time, and became renowned for its V-twins.

The man behind NUT was not its manufacturer. Hugh Mason, who worked in a machine shop for the North Eastern Marine Company, got other people to make bikes to his ideas – first cycle dealer Jock Hall, then an ex-coach builder. All these early machines used bought-in engines, mostly the reliable JAP, and it was a 350 V-twin JAP that Mason rode to victory in the 1913

1928 NUT sidevalve V-twin. This 676cc bike was, like other NUTs, built to a quality rather than down to a price. The Depression put a stop to such high ideals

Junior TT. That brought the orders flooding in, and there were plans for a complete range of 350-775cc JAP machines, roadsters with sidevalves, and ohv racers. After the war, production resumed with an expensive (150 guineas) 500cc tourer, and it looked briefly as if the NUT, with its distinctive cylindrical fuel tank, was to become an established part of the motorcycle scene.

It was not to be, and the next couple of years saw two collapses and subsequent revivals. When the smoke cleared in 1923, NUT settled down to making sports-tourers powered by its own 700cc V-twin, though it has to be said that this engine had much in common with the equivalent JAP. NUTs were never cheap bikes, and the hard years of the late 1920s led the company to offer a 172cc Villiers-powered bike as well. But it was not enough, and in 1933 (after another two address changes) the company disappeared for good.

PANTHER

Panthers, or at least the big thumping sidecar-pulling singles that everyone associates with the name, were unique – there was nothing else quite like them. And though Phelon & Moore dabbled in smaller singles and Villiers-powered commuter bikes, it was the 'Big Pussies' that remained the constant factor, still being churned out of the Cleckheaton works well into the swinging Sixties simply because that was what the company knew best.

Its most distinctive feature came right at the start with founder Joah Phelon's first motorized bicycle. The engine, its cylinder on a forward slope, was a stress-bearing part of the frame, playing the role of front downtube. Stresses were taken by long through-bolts which connected cylinder head to crankcase. In 1924, designer Granville Bradshaw transferred the idea to a 500 ohv single, and the basic Big Pussy had been established – there were no major changes for the next 40 years.

In fact, the 500 very soon became 598cc, which finalized the Panther's engine size almost until the very end. Typically, it had a massive stroke of 100mm, and with 23bhp was designed more with low speed pulling power in mind than anything else. It is hard to believe now, but there was actually a sports version, and the Redwing 90 was a mildly-tuned 500, with twin headlamps and a tank-mounted instrument panel. But the bread-and-butter bikes kept on trickling out of the works, most often with a massive double adult sidecar

attached. While family men wanted something to pull a chair with, there seemed little reason to change anything. In the end, the big single did die, not because P & M thought it was outdated; it was more that component suppliers (notably Burman gearboxes and Lucas magnetos) no longer wanted to make such 'obsolete' parts.

Characteristic pose for a 1954 600cc Panther. By this time, the firm had stopped making little bikes, knowing its forte lay in double-adult sidecar tugs like this one

Panther Model 70 from 1934. This 248cc twin-port bike was the more expensive brother to the Red Panther, the firm's ultra-cheap commuter which saw it through hard times

ROYAL ENFIELD

Royal Enfield of Redditch was not a big company. In fact, compared to the big boys it was quite small – 55,000 bikes were sold to the Forces during the Second World War, when BSA built 425,000. The Bullet, Enfield's best known bike, sold only 9,000 in its 13 year life.

But the company's influence was out of all proportion to its size. For a start, there was a steady stream of innovations in which Enfield was first, or one of the first, on the market. Its first big V-twin in 1912 had a cush hub, a rubber shock absorber in the primary drive, which helped eliminate chain snatch. It featured on all subsequent Enfields except the small ones, and on other makes, of course.

Then there was the little V-twin of the following year; 425cc, ioe valves, and

Royal Enfield is better known for its post-war Bullet and big vertical twins. But in 1922, it was making machines like this elegant V-twin

the first British motorcycle with automatic dry sump lubrication – no longer did the rider have to give a manual squirt of oil every few miles! First too, with a plain big-end bearing in 1935. Chief Designer Tony Wilson-Jones, and continuity of management, were the reason for all this original thinking, and why ideas made it to the production line so fast. The tradition continued after the Second World War with two-way damped telescopic forks in 1946 (well before any of the big three) and a swinging-arm frame for the Bullet three years later. Such advanced suspension at both ends gave the single cylinder Bullet its tremendous success in trials, and Enfield some well-deserved publicity.

In marketing too, Managing Director Major Frank Smith had the foresight to realize that light and nippy 250 singles would take over from the 350/500s; Enfield's range of advanced and powerful (if not always oil-tight) 250cc learner bikes was the result. But it is the Bullet that lives on today, as the Madras-built Indian Enfield.

RUDGE

Our perception of a motorcycle doesn't always accord with reality. But with Rudge, renowned for its sporting (often four-valve) singles, the image is almost right – Rudge-Whitworth, to give it its full name, hardly made anything else. There was the almost obligatory big V-twin in the early days, to placate the sidecar men, and in 1938, just before the firm gave up on motorcycles, a 98cc two-stroke autocycle briefly appeared in the price list.

But above all, Rudge was about single cylinder bikes, which relied on one of two particular innovations with which to mark it out from the competition. Gearing was the first USP (Unique Selling Proposition, a term unknown then, but still relevant). Where other primitive belt-driven singles struggled along with just one ratio (riders had to run alongside on the steeper hills) the Rudge Multi rider had

1938 Rudge Whitworth Special. This is one of the last Coventry-built bikes before production moved down to London

Between the wars, some British manufacturers sought to optimize the four-stroke single with an overhead cam. Rudge favoured four-valves, as on this 500

a choice. The engine and rear wheel pulleys could be expanded or contracted, thus giving infinitely variable gearing, albeit within a limited range. In 1912, it was a great advantage.

But by 1924, the Multi was outdated. Rival bikes had leapfrogged ahead with their separate gearboxes and chain drive, so Rudge decided to catch up in one go. Out went the old ioe engine, infinite gearing and belt drive; in came a four-valve single, four-speed gearbox and chain drive. The public loved it, and factory output doubled to cope with demand. The four-valve 350cc engine was the key. Four valves could draw in more mixture than two, thus giving a bigger bang and more power. So successful was the concept (though Rudge were by no means first) that 250cc and 500 versions followed, as did many successes on race tracks and in the new sport of speedway. Today, few bikes have less than four valves per cylinder, so what would Rudge be building?

SCOTT

There's no denying it, the Scott was different with a capital 'D'. Not only was it a two-stroke (usually the preserve of cheap commuters in pre-war days) but was water-cooled as well. Its almost skimpy, open frame was light, and placed the engine as low as possible for good handling. In the motorcycling world to which the Scott was launched in 1908, sporting contemporaries were its antithesis in just about every way – heavy, big banger four-strokes that needed a firm hand.

Alfred Scott was a highly talented engineer-designer, a lateral thinker who had no great obsession with motorcycles, but realized that the two-stroke twin he had developed for a boat would perform equally well in a two wheeler. That first 333cc engine set the pattern for all Scotts. With its 180-degree crankshaft, high compression and good basic design it was smooth, flexible and fast. And naturally enough, the first Scott motorcycle just bristled with innovations – advanced chain drive where many still used belts, the first foot gearchange and kickstart, and sprung front forks which foreshadowed telescopics.

It was a unique mix of new ideas, but it worked. The 1908 Scott was nimble, quick and stable – it performed so well at an early hillclimb that other manufacturers forced the ACU to handicap it. Once that was lifted, TT wins soon followed. But because it was so different from everything else, riders either loved the Scott, or they didn't. Some would ride nothing else (one racer was moved to say he'd rather lose on a Scott than win on a

LEFT
The Scott's *raison d'être* could not have been more different from the competition, which was why many riders avoided it while others would buy nothing else

RIGHT
Scott rider's view, looking down onto the radiator steering damper and hand gearchange

Norton), while many saw it as a smokey irrelevance which ate spark plugs for breakfast.

The first few years of Scott production seemed to confirm its inventor's brilliance, as he kept coming up with new ideas. There were rotary inlet valves in 1911, which were gear-driven from 1914 – drip lubrication and a unit gearbox also appeared that year. But Alfred Scott seemed to know that he had already come up with an ideal layout for a motorcycle, which couldn't really be improved upon. He turned to other projects, before dying prematurely in 1923.

The 500 and 600cc Squirrel series thrived between the wars (diehards maintained that the original two-speed was the only true Scott), but after 1945, it was a succession of loyal Scott enthusiasts that kept production going in ever more erratic dribs and drabs. Even in the late 1970s, the determined George Silk produced around 140 of his Scott-based 700S, with its modern ancillaries, but familiar-looking two-stroke twin. It was light, nimble and smooth, just like the first Scott. One can't help thinking though, that Alfred Scott today would have been making something far more radical.

SUNBEAM

The mythical 'Gentleman's Motorcycle' has always been a bit like the commuting motorcycle – an attempt (and many have tried) to attract people who would not normally consider a bike, or if they did, would shrink from the loud and rorty performers. But if there was such a thing as a gent's bike, there is a general consensus that Sunbeam was the one.

Its range of small to medium singles in the Twenties and Thirties were not particularly fast or innovative, but they were well finished quality products with price tags to suit. The maker was, in-auspiciously enough, a saucepan maker named John Marston & Co, which produced bicycles from 1890 and its first motorcycle in 1912. From the start, this 350cc side-valve was expensive but well-made, as were the 500 single and JAP/

A Sunbeam S8, part of that search for the elusive 'Gentleman's Motorcycle'. Phil Vincent's efforts were probably closer to the ideal

MAG-engined V-twins which followed. But the Twenties and early Thirties was the heyday of the Marston Sunbeams – well-regarded singles of 250, 350, 500 and 600cc which won the TT in 1920, 1928 and 1929.

But the high price kept sales low, and Sunbeam was taken over in 1937 by AMC (the AJS/Matchless combine). In the middle of the war, the Sunbeam name (all that was left) was sold to BSA. Big BSA's idea was to use the respected moniker to sell its own idea of a gentleman's tourer. The S7 and S8 were certainly tourers, perhaps too much so. The aim was an anglicized BMW, which showed up in the shaft drive, but the rest was sufficiently innovatory to promise a great deal. The in-line twin cylinder engine was all-alloy to reduce weight and aid cooling; its overhead camshaft (very exotic at the time) and short stroke hinted at power. So it was a pity that the prototype vibrated so much that they had to detune it, leaving the Sunbeam with a revvy but fairly gutless motor; hardly the thing for a relaxed gentleman's motorcycle. With their balloon tyres, heavy build and modest power, the last Sunbeam bikes (a short-lived scooter was to follow) were comfortable, but deathly slow. No one really minded when they got the chop in 1956.

BELOW
Thunderbird 650 probably wouldn't have happened but for the power-hungry American market. Appropriately enough, the name came from a Native American legend

TRIUMPH

It's a fair bet that no other motorcycle maker outside Milwaukee has been so discussed, written about and photographed as Triumph. Rather than waffle on about innate character, let's consider why the bikes from Meriden have always

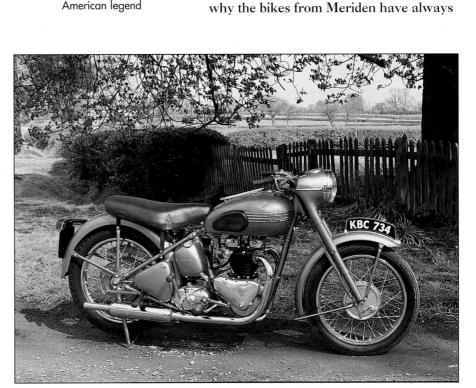

been so appealing. At its best, a Triumph looked terrific – the twins in particular had a simplicity and symmetry that just seemed right; with its tapering fuel tank, the bike's overall proportions were just so, not an ounce of superfluous metal-ware. Triumphs (most of them anyway) were sexy, flash and good-looking. However you wish to describe it, they had style.

The twin cylinder engine was part of the appeal too. It was revvy, powerful and tuneable, in a way that no other twin cylinder engine had been before. Even the multitude of similar (each had its own

LEFT
Sunbeam Model 90, a sidevalve 493cc single in the quality tradition of the old John Marston & Co

foibles) engines dreamt up by the rest of the British industry never really matched it. Of course, it was a bit fragile if worked too hard, and the oil leaks became part of motorcycling folklore. Then there was the inherent vibration which only really became a problem when the 1960s horsepower race began to overstretch a 1930s design.

Whatever the attraction, the Triumph twin was an incredible success. At its peak, it outsold rival BSA by about five to one. So many were sold in the United States that it won the company a Queen's Award for Export. But it is important to realize that this level of commercial success was not reflected in the rest of the range. Triumph certainly made lots of small singles, but the twin culture was inculcated so early that they became relegated to token learner bikes. As for the triples; fast but heavy, and five years too late, they probably drained more from the company coffers than they added.

There is no doubt that the clear-cut virtues and vices of Triumph bikes cannot be separated from those of Edward Turner. Like the bikes, much has been written about Turner. By all accounts, he was the classic flawed genius, capable of great flashes of brilliance as well as fundamental engineering oversights; he knew exactly what the motorcyclist in the street wanted to buy, yet had an autocratic manner; a man of great energy, yet difficult, insecure and a bully. But for the conscientious and supportive team at Meriden, he could never have driven Triumph to the success that he did. (At one time, there were even two sets of engineering drawings kept – one by Turner, who never trained as an engineer and was the mercurial ideas

ABOVE
The Craig Vetter-styled Hurricane was a Trident for America, though based on the BSA with its sloping cylinders. Swoopy glass-fibre and three megaphone silencers transformed the appearance

ABOVE RIGHT
The original Speed Twin of 1937. This engine was the first of a very long line

RIGHT
One of the forgotten bikes from Triumph's twin-centred history. The L2-1 250cc side-valve was good, but too expensive

man rather than the meticulous draughtsman, and the 'proper' corrected set, which were actually used for production. Turner of course, was never told about this, which was probably just as well).

The Triumph story comes in two parts, and all of the above refers to the second half only. The early days were decidedly different. It is odd that Triumph, which came to be seen as the quintessential British bike, was founded by two Germans. Siegfried Bettmann and Maurice Schulte built their first motorcycle in Coventry in 1902. As an aside, such immigrant parentage was not

at all unusual – Bill Harley's parents came from Manchester, Arthur Davidson's from Scotland, and Velocette founder John Goodman was originally Johannes Gujtemann, another German exile.

The first Triumphs had very different priorities to the later ones – no rorty twins, just simple singles which soon became known as 'Trusty Triumphs', because that's what they were. There was nothing very advanced about them, though Bettmann and Schulte did make their own carburettor, and magneto ignition helped. Thirty thousand model Hs were made during the Great War, 550cc single cylinder side-valve bikes with an up-to-the-minute three-speed gearbox, but the old belt final drive. Its spiritual heir was the Model P side-valve, which at £42 or so was cheap enough to help Triumph through the Depression. There were more exciting bikes too, such as the four-valve singles part-designed by Harry Ricardo, which secured several records at Brooklands.

But in the Thirties, Triumph very nearly died. By 1935, the parent company (now mainly concerned with cars) had virtually decided to stop making motorcycles. Ariel head Jack Sangster saved it. He paid just £28,000, and installed Edward Turner as General Manager. But of course, being Turner, the new boss took a hand in just about everything else as well. The first fruits were the Tiger singles. With some mild tuning, a new name, some chrome and bright colours, Turner transformed Triumph's 250, 350 and 500 singles into the Tiger 70, 80 and 90 respectively.

This however was just a foretaste, for in 1937 the Speed Twin was unveiled. It

made a massive impact, simply because it was like nothing else on the market. Most twins were big, heavy things, intended to pull family sidecars. The Speed Twin was as light, slim and manageable as the familiar sports singles, but faster and smoother. It was radical, but not too radical, thus appealing to a basically conservative public – cycle parts came from the existing Tiger 90, and it even looked like a single. The public loved it, and one measure of the Speed Twin's success is that BSA had a prototype twin ready to go for 1940. Within three years of the war's end, every major British manufacturer was making a Speed Twin rival.

Apart from the engine's nature, there was little fundamentally new about it. Both barrel and cylinder head were of cast-iron, and it even used the same bore and stroke measurements as the 250 single. It wasn't over-tuned either, with a single carburettor and modest (7.2:1) compression ratio. On the other hand, all the basics which were to make it so responsive to tuning were there as well: the high-mounted camshafts meant relatively short and stiff pushrods to allow higher revs. And having two cams (one inlet, one exhaust) made it easier to play with the valve timing.

As standard, it gave 27bhp, which was impressive enough at the time. Some people wanted more though, and Triumph responded with the sports Tiger 100 in 1939. Not only did it have more power (33bhp, which often proved too much for the crankshaft) and a 100mph capability, but the Speed Twin's elegant Aramanth Red was swopped for chrome and silver. When the war came, the ohv twins stopped and Triumph devoted itself

TOP
Last Trident was the T160, with many big changes over the original triple. They were actually built at the BSA Small Heath factory by NVT, but sold as Triumphs – confusing!

ABOVE
This 750cc engine was not the final incarnation of the Triumph twin. In 1981, a nice short-stroke 650 was available and at Triumph Meriden's last show it had single and twin carburettor 600s

to churning out the 3HW (a 350 single) for the military. Bombed out of Coventry, it was eventually moved to a greenfield site at Meriden, a village located halfway between Coventry and Birmingham. Said to be the geographical centre of England, Meriden was to be the home of Triumph right up to the end of the old firm.

At first, it was business as usual after the war, with the Speed Twin and Tiger 100 heading up the range. But after six years of financial drain Britain needed exports, and the fastest growing market for British bikes was America. Triumph took advantage of that more than anyone else, leading to accusations (with hindsight) that it became too dependent on a fickle market with a short selling season; too willing to pander to American demands for more and more power. But the point was that Triumph could sell everything it made for America (and at home for that matter) and make a decent profit at the same time.

It was American influence which led Triumph to introduce the Thunderbird, the 650cc version of the Speed Twin. Flat out, this was actually little faster than the Tiger 100, but had far more low speed torque. Still, a more sporting T110 arrived in 1953; like the T100, it still had just one carburettor, but there were plenty of other developments. A swinging arm frame, strengthened bottom end for the engine and an alternator to keep the lights going (the other twins had all-alternator electrics that year). A much modified T110 (the first of the American cigar-shaped record breaking bikes) reached 214.4mph in 1956 at Bonneville with Johnny Allen at the controls.

It was the kudos earned by such records that determined the next twin. The T120 Bonneville of 1959 took the obvious step to twin carburettors, as well as hotter valve timing, to keep up with the demands for more power. Legendary as the Bonneville became (for many people it remains *the* sports twin) it could be seen

TOP
This is the interim Trident, still a T150, but with front disc brake to supersede the original drum

ABOVE
The first Tridents had angular, boxy styling and didn't look like Triumphs at all. This was soon rectified for the American market, as on this export T150, but U.K. buyers had to wait for the T160

as a two-edged sword. Motorcycling was changing – cheap cars lessened its attraction as family transport, and the growth was in ever quicker roadsters for the ton-up boys and Production racers. There is a strong argument that this was where the British industry went wrong, focusing on quick profits by squeezing ever more power out of what were (even then) elderly designs. Nevertheless, a whole generation of motorcyclists, on both sides of the Atlantic, grew up with the Bonneville, which in 750cc form outlasted all other Triumphs.

All this talk of power and speed didn't mean Triumph was ignoring small bikes – many of those Bonnie riders had taken their first wobbling runs on a Tiger Cub. This neat little 200cc single had started out in 1953 as the 150cc Terrier. It lasted until 1968, by which time it was being completely outclassed by the Japanese; a classic case of neglect. It did sell though, which was more than could be said for Edward Turner's other project, the Tigress scooter. With 175cc two-stroke and 250 four-stroke power, it was fast but didn't have the style or nimbleness of the Italian originals, and can be counted as one of Triumph's post-war flops. The same was true of the later T10 scooter, which looked nicer but had fundamental transmission problems, and was really too late to catch the scooter boom in any case.

Meanwhile, there were some at Meriden who realized that the big twins could not go on forever. Particularly if they were expected to wring out another couple of horsepower every year. Bert Hopwood (General Manager at Meriden) and Doug Hele (Head of Development) thought a 750cc three-cylinder was just the thing to leapfrog ahead in the performance game. Based closely on the twin, it could be put on sale fairly quickly, giving Triumph a breathing space in which to develop something genuinely new.

Edward Turner turned it down, but he conveniently retired the year after, leaving the way open. Within a year, the first prototypes were running. With 58bhp at 7,250rpm, they were faster and more powerful than anything else. Unfortunately, Triumph was by now part of the BSA empire, whose waste and lethargy has become a legend in itself. As a result, it took four years for the new Triumph triple to reach the market, at the same time as the disc-braked, overhead cam, electric start Honda CB750. A great opportunity had been wasted.

Nevertheless, the Trident did make a genuine impact. It was just so fast, storming up to 90 or 100mph quicker than anything except a Commando or CB750. It was rather heavy (a long way from the slimline Speed Twin ideal) but handled well, and the sound of the three cylinder engine howling its way up to 8,000rpm was never forgotten. Sad then, that Triumph's industrial troubles kept development down to a minimum. The final T160 of 1975 looked like a real Triumph, and even had an electric start, but by then the Trident was an old bike surviving on borrowed time.

Sadly, the same went for the twins. Through the Sixties there had been gradual improvements, but none of them addressed the fundamental problem of a large vertical twin – vibration. Despite that, in 750cc form the bike kept on selling reasonably well. The worker's co-

T160 and matching sidecar. Part of its svelter look was down to a longer, lower frame, which certainly did the trick

operative at Meriden, which arose out of the 1973 sit-in when NVT tried to close the Triumph factory, actually survived for ten years. There was talk (and even a mock-up) of a new 900cc water-cooled twin, which came to nothing. The real future lay with businessman John Bloor, who bought the name and went on to build thoroughly modern bikes called Triumphs. But that's another story.

VELOCETTE

Three generations of the Goodman family ran Velocette from beginning to end. Johannes Gujtemann was the son of a German merchant; settled in Birmingham he changed his name to first Taylor, then Goodman. His sons Percy and Eugene drove the company between the wars – both were talented design engineers – while their sister Ethel acted as buyer, later Sales Director. And *their* sons (Bertie and Peter) kept things going for the last two decades.

Yet despite the continuity of ownership (a rarity in itself among British bike firms) there was a curious internal split within the family. Well, not a split exactly, for the two sides seem to have co-existed amiably enough. But while Percy Goodman wanted to build racing singles, Eugene was set on that other (probably more elusive) pursuit, the everyman bike, for people who were not motorcyclists by nature. What united them was a commitment to high-quality engineering, whether applied to a utility two-stroke or overhead cam racer.

Despite the high profile of the Velocette singles, the company started out with far more humble machines. Like many motorcycle makers, the company began with bicycles, though unlike the others there was no smooth progression through motorized pushbikes to the final product. Veloce Ltd. (as it later became) experimented with roller skates, a 20hp car, and even exported rickshaws to the Far East! But an advanced little 276cc unit construction two-wheeler, and a more conventional 500, convinced the Goodmans that their future lay in motorcycles.

It was the 200/250cc two-strokes from 1913 which established Velocette.

Firmly in the everyman mould, they were well made, economical and cheap (just £38 for the Light Two-Fifty). Things changed in 1925, when the family firm's other stroke of inspiration manifested itself. Percy Goodman came up with a beautiful little overhead cam 350, first bike in the long-running K-series. Alec Bennett won the 1926 Junior TT on one, a full ten minutes ahead of his nearest rival. Suddenly, everyone wanted a Velocette. The Goodmans moved to a bigger factory and dropped the two-strokes, though they later returned by popular demand.

But despite the success, it was clear to Eugene that Veloce could not survive on racing wins alone. The result was the high-camshaft M-series, which became the definitive British sports single. Cheaper and easier to build than the ohcs, they were almost as fast, thanks to the short and stiff pushrods which permitted more revs and hence more power. The first 250 MOV was swiftly followed by a 350, the MAC, and a 500 MSS, and it was this layout which Velocette stuck with right through to the end in 1971. There were experiments, of course, notably with DOHC, rotary valves and of course the supercharged 'Roarer' racer twin. But the high-cam ohvs performed so well there seemed little reason to change them. Their excellent performance endeared them to committed clubmen everywhere, but their idiosyncracies did not.

But the dream of an everyman bike would not go away, and in 1948 the LE arrived. Probably the most docile and unassuming motorcycle ever made, it was a water-cooled flat twin with side valves and very little power. The theory

The ultimate Velocette in 1938 was this KSS, derived directly from the racers. The Mk2 shown here used an alloy cylinder head

was that its exceptional quietness, leg-shields and car-style gearchange would appeal to the non-motorcyclist. Alas, the commuters did not see it that way, though the police bought enough to keep production going right to the end.

Velocette's overhead cam engine did great things for the company in the Twenties, but the pushrod M-series was nearly as fast, and cheaper to make

VINCENT

Imagine a motorcycle with a top speed of 125mph and easy 100mph cruising. Nought to sixty takes about 6 seconds. Comfort and convenience are central design aims. With excellent handling and full weather protection, it's a superb long distance mile eater. It isn't cheap (costing about the same as a small car) but it is the ultimate. It all sounds pretty modern, but the Vincent was offering all of this in 1955, and most of it even before the Second World War.

Such performance is impressive enough now, but must have seemed stratospheric 40 or 50 years ago, when Vincent V-twins offered the speed of a racer combined with long-running stamina and very high quality. In so many ways, the Vincent really was out on its own.

Black Lightning V-twin engine in all its glory. It was the most powerful Vincent of all, with 70bhp at 5,600rpm and a claimed maximum of 150mph

Although the Lightning was the ultimate Vincent, far more touring Rapides (45bhp) and sporting Black Shadows (55bhp) were made. A Shadow could outrun anything on the road in any case

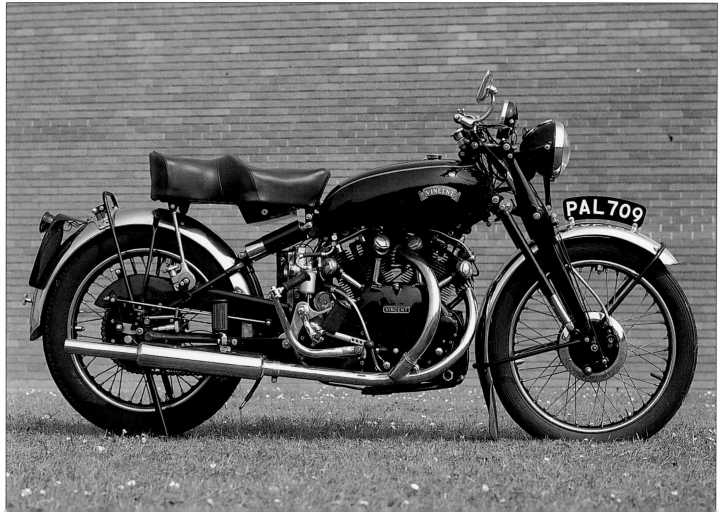

Philip Vincent was an idealist in the way that George Brough was. Like Brough, he wanted to create the ultimate luxury high-speed motorcycle. Unlike Brough, he came up with many innovations which made the Vincent far more than just a fast, well-made V-twin. As an engineer, he was supremely gifted. At the age of 17 he had designed the cantilever rear suspension which was to feature on all Vincents. Hub centre steering, monoshock suspension and an hydraulic clutch were just some of the items he designed which never became part of the Vincent motorcycle. But in collaboration with Australian Phil Irving he achieved his ideal, even if in the end there were not enough people prepared to pay for it.

There were Vincents before the vees though. In 1927, PCV (his initials became the common form of address) borrowed enough money from his father to buy the HRD name. The next few years saw a variety of Vincent-HRDs leave the Old North Road works in Stevenage, most of them powered by JAP singles; but all had Vincent's own cantilever rear suspension. At a time when most motorbikes had no rear springs of any kind, such an innovation was viewed with suspicion. Competition success helped overcome it, but the real breakthrough came in 1934. JAP stopped making a suitable engine, and within three months, Phil Irving had produced a Vincent-HRD single to replace it. A couple of years later, it occurred to Irving that two such singles would make a much faster V-twin, for a modest re-tooling cost.

The resulting Vincent-HRD Rapide Series 'A' laid down the basis for all

The author enjoys pretending to be in charge of a Vincent Black Prince, which really belongs to Bernard Davenport

succeeding Vincent vee-twins. Its 998cc engine produced 45bhp, enough for 108mph once run in. There were alloy cylinders to keep the weight down and aid cooling, and high-mounted camshafts (just like the single). And it was housed in a sprung frame, of course, which made the Rapide very nimble at a time when most V-twins were heavy, ponderous things used for pulling sidecars around. Of course, Vincent V-twins often had chairs attached too, but they pulled them faster than anything else.

The post-war 'B' series Rapide added another innovation. Out went the conventional tubular frame, in came the engine as a stressed member, hung from a box-section beam which doubled as the oil tank. It also had unit construction (years before the big factories moved to it *en masse*) and a new, strong gearbox (because the old separate Burman gearbox wasn't always up to an engine of such unaccustomed power). As development continued, there were innumerable details which pointed to the

There were also some useful mechanical updates underneath the bodywork of the 'D' series V-twins, the most significant of which was coil ignition. The engine came in Rapide (as the Black Knight) or tuned Shadow (Black Prince) form

designers' aim, not just for the fastest bike you could buy, but the most convenient as well. The dual seat, for example, was adjustable for height, and the gearchange for length as well. Adjusting the chain needed no tools; all that was necessary was to loosen the wheel spindle on its integral tommy bar, and turn the big knurled adjuster by hand. Buyers of the later enclosed bikes did not need to hoist it onto an awkward centre stand – a long lever made things easy.

This convenience engineering reached its height in the Series 'D' Black Prince and Black Knight. Full bodywork to enclose the engine and protect the rider was Phil Vincent's idea of what the gentleman motorcyclist should be riding. It had much in common with Edward Turner's attempts at about the same time to sanitize and clean up the Triumph twins. But both missed the point. The fact that the engine, with its fins, hunks of alloy and suggestion of power was visible, was all part of the appeal not only of Vincents and Triumphs, but of any motorcycle. In any case, Vincents were still very expensive, and it seemed

there just weren't enough gentleman motorcyclists around. Production ceased in December 1955.

Black Prince riders didn't get the big and beautiful 150mph Smith speedometer which dominated the outlook from a Black Shadow. In fact, it all looks a bit sparse for a luxury tourer

ZENITH

Some companies had one good idea, and stuck to it – Scott's water-cooled two-stroke is one example, the sidecar-pulling Big Pussy Panther another. Zenith's misfortune was that its own Big Idea was overtaken by events after a comparatively brief glimpse of glory.

It was the Gradua, an ingenious means of obtaining variable gear when other bikes were usually stuck with just one ratio; even if they had a choice, it entailed stopping to fiddle with belts and pulleys. But once that idea had had its day, Zenith appeared to relapse into relative obscurity. It never built its own engines, and tended to follow fashion rather than lead it. Sloping cylinders arrived in the late 1920s and saddle tanks and foot gearchanges in the early 1930s, but only because everyone else was doing the same.

The Gradua system (seen here on a JAP-powered Brooklands racer) gave Zenith a massive advantage when racing against the fixed gear bikes, until multi-speed gearboxes came along

The Gradua was not Zenith's first bike. That came three years earlier, and it was far from conventional. Named the Bicar, it featured hub centre steering and, instead of a motorcycle-style frame, a horizontal tubular chassis. Among the options was a two-guinea bucket seat in place of the saddle; this was more like a two-wheeled car.

But things changed when designer Fred Barnes joined the company in 1907. His new Zenette used a 500cc Fafnir engine (similar to the Bicar's) but had more conventional front forks (from Druid) and soon had the option of Gradua gears. To change ratio, the rider turned a wheel which moved the sides of the engine pulley in or out, thus altering its diameter. The Gradua's trick was to move the rear wheel backwards or forwards in the frame at the same time as the pulley shifted. This kept the drive belt in constant tension and meant changes could be made on the move.

In days when, faced with a hill,

riders had to either get pedalling, run alongside the machine or stop to swap pulleys, it was high-tech indeed. It also gave Zenith a massive advantage in hillclimbs. So massive, that the authorities took the familiar step of banning it to give the others a chance. The factory turned this to its advantage by using the word 'Banned' as its slogan, thus attributing to Graduas a hint of the forbidden.

Unfortunately, this moment of notoriety could not last. Even as the Gradua ban came into force in 1910, there were the first signs of all-chain drive and proper gearboxes. Zenith's variable ratios went on selling for a while though, such was its reputation; a V-

Zenith's Big Idea, the Gradua. This is a 550cc V-twin from 1914

twin version succeeded the single, and a 'Coffee grinder' handle took over from the wheel (said to be an old bicycle chainwheel with the teeth turned off!)

Other, more conventional Zeniths, appeared after the belt-drive Gradua's demise in 1926. All used bought-in engines, mostly JAP singles and V-twins, and none was really that distinguished, though privateers like Joe Wright secured a number of speed records on the rortier bikes. Joe managed 150.736mph on a refurbished, supercharged Zenith racer in 1930. But the glory days were over, and apart from 250 JAP sidevalve V-twins assembled in the late 1940s, Zenith's career ended when the Second World War began.

Index

Page numbers in italics refer to illustrations

Agasta, Count Domenico 52, 53
AJS 8, 9, *9*
      Luxury Sports 10
      Porcupine 10
AJS/Matchless 9
AMC (Associated Motor Cycles) 9,
      48
American Machine and Foundry
      Company 34
Ariel 6, *6*, 7, 56
      Huntmaster *6*, 7, 8
      Mk II Square Four *7*, 8
      KH 8
Aston Martin 37
Austin Seven 12

Barnes, Fred 78
Barter, W.J. 19
Baughman, Wayne 43
Bayliss, Thomas & Co 22
Bettman, Siegfried 69
Birmingham Small Arms Company
      15, 17
BMW 10
      R32 10
      R69S 11, *11*
      R90/S Racer *11*
Boanerges 13
Bonneville 71
Bradshaw, Granville 62
Brampton Biflex forks 13
Brockhouse Engineering 43
Brough, George 12, 13, 76
Brough Superior 12, 13, 14, 44
      SS80 *12*, 13, *13*
      SS100 13, *13*
Brough, William 12
BSA 8, 14, *14*, 15, *15*, 55, 63, 68,
      68, 72
      A7 14, 16
      A10 16
      A60/A65 16
      B31 15
      B32 15
      Bantam 14, 15, 54
      Blue Star 15
      Empire Stars 15
      Golden Flash 16
      Gold Star 14, 16, *17*
      M20 14
      M21 15
      Road Rocket 16
      Rocket Gold Star 16
      Rocket Three *14*, *15*, *16*, 17
      Sloper 15
      Trident 17
Burman gearbox 62, 77

Clady Ulster GP 10
Collier, Charlie 8, 48
Collier, Harry 8, 48
Craig, Joe 58

Davidson, Arthur 25, 41
Davidson, Walter 26
Davidson, William C. 26

Davison, Willie G. 34
De Dion engine 6
DKW 15, 32
Douglas 18, *18*, 55
      Dragonfly *18*
      Model E *18*, *19*
Ducati 19, *19*, 20, *20*, 21
      Darmah 900 21
      864cc Desmodromic *19*
      750GT 21
      2550 Mach 1 20
      Pantah 21
      750SS 21
      900SS 21

Earles forks 11, 53
Excelsior 22, *22*
      Auto-byk 22
      Manxman 22, *22*
      Schwinn 23

Ford, Henry 25
      Model T 25, 26
Fowler, Rem 57
Franklin, Charles 42
Friz, Max 10

Gilera 10, *52*, *53*
Goodman, John 69, 73
Goodman, Percy 73, 74
Gustafson, Charlie 41

Hailwood, Mike 20
Handley, Wal 15
Harley-Davidson 10, 21, 23, 24,
      24, 25, 26, 27, 28, *28*, 29,
      29, 30, *31*, 32, *32*, *33*, 34,
      34, 35, *35*, 36, 41, 43
      Duo Glide 31, *35*
      Kucklehead 30, 31
      Panhead 30, *32*
      Silent Gray Fellow *26*
      Sportster 31, *35*
      Super Glide 34
      WLA 31
      WLC *32*
Harley, William 25, 69
Hedstrom, Oscar 38, 40, 43
Hele, Doug 71
Henderson 36, *36*
      Henderson 4 *36*
Henderson, Tom William G. 36
Hesketh 37, *37*
      V1000 37
Honda 15, 24, 32, 47, 49, 72
      CB77
      Superdream 24
Hopwood, Bert 16, 56, 58, 71
Hummer 32
Hutton, Fred 55
Indian 23, 27, 29, 31, 36, 38, 40,
      40, 41, *41*, 42, *42*, 43
      Ace *38*
      Big Chief 42
      Brave 43
      Chief 42
      Indian Chief 80 *39*
      Junior Scout 42
      ME-125 43
      Powerplus 41

Scout 42
Sport Scout 43

Irving, Phil 76

James 44, *44*
      Derby 44
      Minerva 44
      Safety 44
      Super Sports *44*
Janecek, Frantisek 45
JAP engine *12*, 13, 61, 66
Jawa 45, *45*
      Jawa 500 *45*
John Marston & Co 66
Jozif, Josef 46
Laverda 47, *47*
      750GTL 47

Lawrence T.E. *13*
Leader/Arrow 6, 8
Le Vack, Bert 55

MAG 6
Mason, Hugh 61
Matchless 8, 48, *48*
      G50 48
      G80 *48*
      Silver Arrow 48
      Silver Hawk 48
McCandless, Rex 59
Meccanica Verghera 53
Minarelli engine 43
Mockett, John 37
Mole, Vic 6
Monza GP 20
Morini 49, *49*, 50
Morini, Alfonso 49
Guzzi, Carlo 50
Motto Guzzi 21, 50, *50*, 51, *51*
Moto-Rêve 57
      V7 Sport *50*
MV 52, *52*, 53, *53*, 54, *54*
      MV600 roadster *54*
      750S *52*

New Hudson 55, *55*
New Imperial 56, *56*
North Eastern Marine Company
      61
Norton 14, 47, 56, *56*, 57, *57*, 58,
      58, 59, *59*, 60, *60*, 65
      Big Four 57
      Commando 58, 60, *60*, 72
      Dominator 58, *58*
      Featherbed 59, 60
      16H 58
      Manxman 58, *59*
      Model 30
Norton, James Lansdowne 57
NUT 61, *61*

Page, Val 6, 7, 8
Panther 62, *62*
      Red Panther *62*
      Redwing 90
Parodi, Giorgio 51
Patchett, George-William 45
Perrey, Harold 6
Phelon & Moore 62

Pridmore, Reg *11*

Ravelli, Jean 51
Red Hunter engine 6, 7
Remor, Pietro 53
Ricardo, Harry 69
Rolls-Royce 12, 13
Royal Enfield 63, *63*
      Bullet 63, *63*
Rudge 64, *64*
Rudge-Whitworth 64
      Rudge-Whitworth Special
      64

Sangster, Jack 6, 56
Schulte, Maurice 69
Scott 65, *65*, 66
      Squirrel series 66
Scott, Alfred 65, 66
Selly Oak Factory 8
Silk, George 66
Small Heath works 8
Smith, Major Frank 63
Square Four 6, 7
Stevens, Albert John 8
Strugis rally 24
Sturmely-Archer gearbox 13
Sunbeam 66, *66*
      Model 90 *67*
      S8 *66*

Taglioni, Fabio 20, 21
Tonti, Lino 51
Triumph 6, 14, 16, 17, 31, 47, 49,
      56, 67, *67*, 68, *68*, 69, *69*,
      70, *70*, 71, *71*, 72, *72*, 78
      Hurricane (Trident U.S.) *68*
      Speed Twin *68*, 70, 72
      Terrier 71
      Thunderbird 650 67, 71
      Tiger 90 70
      Tiger Cub 54, 71
      Tigresse 71
      Trident *70*, 71, 72
Turner, Edward 6, 7, 56, 58, 68, 71,
      72, 78

Veloce Ltd. 73
Velocette 6, 69, 73, *73*, 74, *74*
Villiers 6, 62
Vincent 75, *75*, 76, *76*, 77, *77*, 78,
      78
      Black Knight 77
      Black Lightning *75*
      Black Prince *76*, 78
      Black Shadow *75*, *76*, 78
      Rapide *75*, 76, 77
Vincent, Philip 76

Welake 37
White and Poppe 6
Williams, Peter 56
Wilson-Jones, Tony 63

Yamaha 32

Zanghi, Phillip 43
Zenith, 78, *78*, 79, *79*
      Gradua 79, *79*